A LIFE OF ST. BENEDICT

MAN OF BLESSING

CARMEN ACEVEDO BUTCHER

PARACLETE PRESS
BREWSTER, MASSACHUSETTS

Man of Blessing: A Life of St. Benedict

2006   First Printing

Copyright 2006 by Carmen Acevedo Butcher

ISBN 1-55725-485-0

          Library of Congress Cataloging–in–Publication Data
Butcher, Carmen Acevedo.
  Man of Blessing : a life of Saint Benedict / by Carmen Acevedo
Butcher.
     p. cm.
  Includes bibliographical references.
ISBN 1-55725-485-0
1.Benedict, Saint, Abbot of Monte Cassino. 2. Christian saints—
Italy—Biography. I. Title.
  BR1720.B45B88 2006
   271'.102—dc22   2005035827
10 9 8 7 6 5 4 3 2 1

Published by Paraclete Press
Brewster, Massachusetts
www.paracletepress.com

Printed in the United States of America

This humble volume is dedicated to the brothers and sisters who serve in the Benedictine family in ways as diverse as they are, both inside and outside the walls of monasteries, all over this colorful globe, and also to their associates, the oblates who "offer" themselves to the Benedictine ideal of peace in a world that needs them. They bless us daily.

And for the unforgettable fragrance of Benedictine hospitality, *ora et labora*, and *pax*, special thanks go to my Benedictine friends at the St. Walburg Monastery (http://www.stwalburg.org/), Sisters Deborah Harmeling, Mary Tewes, and Teresa Wolking, as well as to Sisters Linda Kulzer (St. Benedict's Monastery) and Judith Sutera (Mount St. Scholastica). They have answered my questions patiently, and they have made St. Benedict very real to me by living lives of kindness that sparkle with inclusion.

"The finest and noblest characters prefer

a life of dedication to a life of self-indulgence."

—Cicero

We honor Saint Benedict who advocated justice

for each person,

but especially for the poor and powerless.

May we learn to live simply

and share with those less fortunate.

Bless us with a sense of justice

tempered with mercy.

We ask this through Jesus, the Christ,

both now and forever. Amen.

—from *A Prayer for the Feast of Saint Benedict,* July 11

CONTENTS

THE ALPS

Milano

Po

Adda

APENNINE MOUNTAINS

Ravenna

Rubicon

BENEDICT'S ITALY

Pisae

Florentia

Mount
Sibillini
Range

UMBRIA

Spoleto

Tiber

Nursia

Subiaco

ADRIATIC SEA

Anio

Roma

Enfide

Cassinium &
Monte Cassino

Tarracina

Capua

Neopolis

Pompeii

TYRRHENIAN SEA

SICILY

SICILIAN
SEA

0   75   150   225 Kilometers

0   50   100   150 Miles

PREFACE

What's in a name? In a faith predicated on the Word of John 1:1, everything. The Bible emphasizes the power of everything to do with language, and if we read the Old and New Testaments with an eye for acts of naming, the meanings of names, and especially name changes (of the sort a cardinal experiences when he is elected pope), God's goodness and the blessing of divine salvation come into focus.

One of the first object lessons in Scripture teaches the authority associated with naming. God brings the freshly created livestock, wild animals, and birds to Adam for him to christen, a potent symbol of our responsibility for the earth and all its creatures. Later, the name *Abraham,* for "father *(abh)* of a multitude *(raham),*" represents the divine calling of this first Hebrew patriarch. Then Jacob (the "heel-grabber," he who will "trip you up") cheats his brother, Esau, out of his birthright, but at Peniel, the trickster wrestles with a significantly *unnamed*, mysterious and powerful heavenly creature who then re-names Jacob "Israel," or *yisra'el* in the Hebrew, from *sara,* "he fought with" and *El,* "God." The new moniker suggests this Hebrew leader has come to grips with himself and his identity in God and will now lead a holy life.

Something similar happens to the mercurial fisherman named Simon (from the Hebrew *Shim'on* for "hearing"). He seems open to and swayed by whatever he may be "hearing" or "listening" to at the moment, as his betrayal of Jesus shows, but after Jesus christens Simon "Peter," he does become the "rock" or "stone" on which the Church of peace is built, according to Matthew's Gospel, chapter sixteen. Biblical authors are also keen to emphasize that the meaning of the common Jewish name *Jesus* originates in *Yeshua,* for "God saves."

To ancient minds, a word is no mere shallow label. A name more than identifies a person to the world; it is seen as mysteriously participating in the essence of whatever it represents. It *is* what it symbolizes. Words connect visible, specific people-and-things with the invisible, universal reality. Put another way, words are not simply useful identifiers (like the two inch x three inch address tags we affix to luggage)—they are expressions of ultimate meaning. Therefore, when the poetic John names Jesus "the Word" in the first chapter of his Gospel, the words themselves in that phrase, "the Word," are felt to be the "Logos," "Jesus," "Love" in an immediate, mystical way perhaps lost on our modern minds.

More than a handle for saying "Hello," then, a name defines and encourages. A good name can remind a discouraged soul of his or her best self. On dark days, I am thankful for the light of my first name, *Carmen,* meaning "song" or "poem"; and on sunny blue-sky days when all goes well, my name prompts me to praise God for His good gifts. I am surprised when I survey an American college classroom that out of twenty brimming-with-potential students, only two or three hands go up to show they know the significance of their names. In my experience, the meaning of a well-chosen name is something a soul can steep in for a lifetime of good and bad days.

With this importance of names in mind, we can explore why the 265th Holy Father, the former Cardinal Joseph Alois Ratzinger, chose "Benedict" as the name under which he will serve as head of a Christian Church with one billion diverse followers. *Benedict* is a powerful name, with an equally powerful history, starting in the fifth century AD with St. Benedict, and it now guides a pope already aptly named at birth. Recognizing the deep resonances in this regnal name choice requires that we first understand the several names Pope Benedict XVI received at birth.

On Holy Saturday, April 16th, 1927, in a little village in Upper Bavaria called Marktl am Inn ("Little Market on the Inn River"), two proud new parents, Joseph Ratzinger, Sr., a police officer, and his wife, Mary, name their youngest child *Joseph*. In Hebrew, *Joseph* means "God will give more," a phrase expressing their gratitude to God for this little baby, their latest "present" (or "blessing") from the loving, generous God who always will "give more."

God's spiritual and physical gifts to us are often called "blessings," and the parents of the future pope know that *Joseph* will constantly remind their son of the unending nature of God's openhandedness. Although God shows His love to us daily by presenting us with many good blessings—ace health, eyesight, three meals of nourishing food, kind family and friends, and peace—these are easy enough to overlook and take for granted, but having a name that means "blessing" is in itself a blessed prompt to be grateful.

For Pope Benedict XVI, his given name Joseph is also a solid link between both his heavenly Father and his earthly *Vater,* and his Christian name must remind him of the way community is made possible when there is harmony between the divine and the ordinary. His devout parents knew Joseph is a good spiritual legacy for a newborn, because it is also the name of Jacob's favorite son who, learning humility and forgiveness, matures into a great leader in Egypt, a unifier during difficult famine years (see Genesis 41). Adding to the richness of the pope's initial christening, his middle name is Alois, German for "wisdom"; and Ratzinger suggests "good counsel," for the masculine German noun *Rat* means "advice."

This native background for Joseph Alois Ratzinger becomes even more interesting when we consider that his regnal choice, *Benedict*, means "to speak well of, to praise," from the Latin *benedicere* (*bene-* for "well," and the root, *dicere*, for "to speak"). Another synonym for *benedicere* is "to bless," making the Latin *Benedict* very complementary with the Hebrew *Joseph* ("God will give more"), because both emphasize the idea of "blessing," but with a difference. *Benedict's* etymology is rooted in *dicere* ("to speak"), focusing on the necessity in a loving, peaceful community of well-chosen words and right speech, as discussed in the third chapter of the Epistle of James, from the New Testament: "Anyone who makes no mistakes in speaking is perfect, able to keep the whole body in check with a bridle."

This verse takes on added meaning when we remember that a blessing or a curse meant more to a person alive in Benedict's day. If a neighbor blessed you, you took that verbal goodwill very seriously, convinced it would make something positive happen in your life; conversely, a neighbor's curse was considered a death knell for whatever in your life had been damned. The word and the action were believed to have an if-then relationship. Modern psychology is beginning to rediscover this ancient truth, and we all recognize (on a daily basis) the profound ways others' words influence us in the nitty-gritty of our lives, for good and for ill.

This truth is obvious if we look at how we use corporeal images to describe speech. We give someone a compliment, describing it as a "pat on the back." We talk of "stroking" someone's ego. Criticism, on the other hand, is a verbal "lashing," and we all know a "harsh" word from someone comes as a "blow" to the self. The very physicality of these phrases shows we instinctively grasp the soul-building or soul-crushing power of words.

This profound linguistic history of *bless* is not lost on someone as learned as the former Cardinal Joseph Ratzinger, and when Pope John Paul II died on April 2nd, 2005, Ratzinger paid homage to his close friend eloquently, several times emphasizing the power of speech and the action of "blessing":

> None of us can ever forget how in that last Easter Sunday of his life, the Holy Father, marked by suffering, came once more to the window of the Apostolic Palace

and one last time gave his *blessing* "urbi et orbi." We can be sure that our beloved Pope is standing today at the window of the Father's house, that he sees us and *blesses* us. Yes, *bless* us, Holy Father. We entrust your dear soul to the Mother of God, your Mother, who guided you each day and who will guide you now to the eternal glory of her Son, our Lord Jesus Christ. [Author's emphasis.]

Less than two weeks later, on April 19th, Cardinal Ratzinger was elected Bishop of Rome, adopting the name Benedict XVI, and on April 24th, Benedict XVI was formally inaugurated as pope. Three days later, he held his first general audience in St. Peter's Square, and with some 15,000 people present, he explained his choice of names:

I wish to speak of the name I chose on becoming bishop of Rome and pastor of the universal Church. I chose to call myself Benedict XVI ideally as a link to the venerated Pontiff, Benedict XV, who guided the Church through the turbulent times of the First World War. He was a true and courageous prophet of peace who struggled strenuously and bravely, first to avoid the drama of war and then to limit its terrible consequences. In his footsteps I place my ministry, in the service of reconciliation and harmony between peoples, profoundly convinced that the great good of peace is above all a gift of God, a fragile and precious gift to be invoked, safeguarded, and constructed, day after day and with everyone's contribution. The name *Benedict* also evokes the extraordinary figure of the great "patriarch of western monasticism," St. Benedict of Nursia. The progressive expansion of the Benedictine Order which he founded exercised an enormous influence on the spread of Christianity throughout the European continent. For this reason, St. Benedict is much venerated in Germany, and especially in Bavaria, my own land of origin; he constitutes a fundamental point of reference for the unity of Europe and a powerful call to the irrefutable Christian roots of European culture and civilization.

Pope Benedict XVI says he chose "Benedict" because it is a name associated with two Christians who worked for global peace: Pope Benedict XV and St. Benedict. His first-year headlines confirm this papal focus on blessing and reconciliation: "Pope reaches out to Orthodox Church in inaugural pilgrimage" (CBC News, Canada); "Pope preaches unity in first official trip" (Myrtle Beach *Sun News);* "Pope seeks closer ties with other churches" *(International Herald Tribune);* "Pope gives Chinese priests warm welcome" *(Chicago Tribune);* "Pope and reformist Father Hans Küng have "friendly" meeting, Vatican says" (Catholic News Service); and "Pope Benedict XVI Hails IRA Disarmament Decision" *(The Conservative Voice).* He is concentrating his efforts on living out the truth of his name.

This truth was first established in ancient Italy by St. Benedict of Nursia.

INTRODUCTION

Benedict's life was a series of risings in the dark. Many times in the profound stillness after midnight, under the black, frosty skies of early winter, while most Italians, peasants, politicians, children, fishermen, high-born ladies, servants, teachers, and bakers were sound asleep, lights fired up in the monasteries, and the man in a tunic began his day with a psalm: *Domine, labia mea aperies, et os meum annuntiabit laudem tuam* ("O Lord, open my lips, and my mouth will declare your praise"—Psalm 51:15).

It was not yet 2 AM when this monk sat up and tapped himself gently on the forehead, sternum, and left and right shoulders, using the sign of the cross to invoke the Holy Trinity for spiritual protection. In the unheated room, the stone floor against his feet likely jolted him awake, and he squinted for his night shoes, bending over to feel for them at the foot of his cot. Finding them and slipping each on, thankful in the darkness for their warmth, he headed to chapel for Vigils. By 5 AM, this Benedictine abbot had already spent nearly three hours engaged in communal prayer and the recitation of psalms called the Opus Dei, or "the Work of God," also known as the Divine Office. This singing is still the heart of Benedictine life.

In a fourth-century letter, Alexandrine Bishop St. Athanasius voiced this medieval view on the significance of holy singing:

That which causes grief is healed when we sing psalms, and that which causes stumbling will be discovered. Those who do not recite the divine songs in this manner do not sing them wisely. They bring delight to themselves, but they incur blame, because a hymn of praise is not suitable on the lips of a sinner. The Psalms are not recited with melodies because of a desire for pleasant sounds. Rather, this is a sure sign of the harmony of the soul's reflections.[3]

St. Athanasius also suggests that hearing the psalms strengthens the soul in a trinity of ways: The singer learns the facts of Biblical history and prophecy; the Psalter nurtures the emotions; and the psalms deepen the listener's understanding of the Bible's words and of God, because he or she participates intimately in the act of listening. "And the one who hears is deeply moved, as though he himself were speaking, and is affected by the words of the songs, as if they were his own songs."[4]

After the singing of Vigils, the medieval monk turned to his second most important activity, *lectio divina,* or spiritual reading. In his *Rule,* Benedict did not define or describe this common practice because it was such an intrinsic part of monastic life. Manuscripts were at a premium, and the monk's main duty was to be a keen listener to God's word; therefore, these times of "spiritual reading" meant more than simply reading the Holy Scriptures. The monk memorized as much of them as possible, internalizing their verses deep into his very marrow by quietly repeating them over and over. He steeped his soul in the Bible by meditating on the verses as he learned them, until he was led into prayer.

At daybreak (about 6 AM in winter), the monk then chanted Matins ("morning") and Lauds ("to praise"), and when daylight was full, about 6:45 AM, the Divine Office called Prime ("the first hour") started. From 7:30 AM until 8 AM, there was a brief time for reading, writing, or other duties. Next, the monk changed his shoes and washed his face before returning to the oratory to begin singing Terce ("the third hour"), followed by Morrow Mass and the Chapter of Faults. At the daily Chapter, breaches of regular discipline were confessed or alleged, and corrected, general announcements were made, and a blessing was pronounced on the day's work.

From 9:45 AM until 12:30 PM, the morning was filled with a period dedicated to work, either intellectual, educational, manual, administrative, or service-oriented. Then the community came together to recite Sext ("the sixth hour"), followed by the sung High Mass. About 1:30 PM, Nones ("the ninth hour") was celebrated. Around 2 PM, some twelve hours after rising, the monks ate their one simple meal of the day. If there were guests, they would break bread with the abbot.

The second period of *lectio divina* was enjoyed after dinner and lasted from about 3 PM until 5 PM. Then came Vespers ("evening" prayer; also called "evensong," from the native Old English word, *æfen-sang)*. After this celebration, the monk shuffled into his night shoes and performed the Maundy. This is the ritual washing of the monks' feet in memory of Christ, who washed the feet of His disciples. A drink of wine in the refectory refreshed him next before he heard a short public reading in choir, followed about 6:15 PM by the celebration of Compline (from the Latin *completorium* or "complement"). Just before 7 PM, he retired to the dormitory for seven good hours of sleep before rising again.

Several times every day, he and his brothers stopped their lives and gathered to recite Matins, Lauds, Prime, Terce, Sext, None, Vespers, and Compline. By week's end, they had prayed their way through the entire Latin Psalter of 150 Old Testament Psalms. And each week, as designated in chapter sixty-six of Benedict's *Rule*, the monks read from its wisdom, "so that none of the brethren may excuse himself on the ground of ignorance."

This once rather obscure Italian abbot whose short *Rule* is now the solid foundation of Western monasticism remains, for the most part, an elusive figure historically. His exact chronology is impossible to nail: Its dates are predominantly scholars' best guesses, but the peaceful tenor of this monk's life is unmistakable through over 1,400 years of telling it.

CHRONOLOGY

St. Benedict's Italy is an unstable province of a collapsing Roman Empire. Throughout the fifth century after the birth of Christ, waves of invaders weaken the peninsula. First, Goth warriors march along the Via Flaminia and into Rome, sacking it in 410. Others soon follow.

c. 480 AD. Into this fragile, violent world, Benedict (or "Bennet") is born in Nursia, among the Apennine valleys and mountains of central Italy. He begins life as the son of a lesser Roman nobleman *(liberiori genere,* "of good birth"). Tradition gives him a twin sister, Scholastica. This is also the agreed-upon year for the birth of the highborn Roman Boëthius, author of *Consolation of Philosophy.* During Benedict's earliest years, the half-Hun, half-Scirian chieftain, Odoacer, calls himself *Rex Italiae (King of Italy).*

489. Theodoric the Great invades Italy. He has been invited to do so by the Eastern Roman Emperor Zeno, who wants Odoacer forced out.

493. Theodoric founds the Ostrogothic kingdom in Italy. His thirty-plus years in power are relatively stable. Also, young Benedict leaves Nursia with his family to spend his teenage years attending Rome's schools for classical studies, until about 499.

c. 500. Benedict abandons Rome and with his loyal nurse moves forty miles east to Enfide (the contemporary Affile). Benedict works his first miracle here. Gregory's record of

Benedict's miracles may stymie the modern sensibility, but his audience found them comforting, not troubling. The medieval acceptance of divine supernatural acts will be discussed in chapter one.

c. 501. This miracle brings Benedict local fame; to escape it, he heads for Subiaco, on the Anio River, and meets Romanus, a monk from a nearby monastery.

c. 502–505. Young Benedict lives as a hermit *(eremos,* "desert") in a cave. Romanus shares food with him.

c. 506. Monks from the nearby monastery of Vicovaro ask Benedict to be their abbot. When they try to poison him, he returns to his cave in Subiaco.

c. 507–529. Benedict teaches the gospel to those who flock to him at Subiaco, and performs miracles. To house these followers, he builds thirteen monasteries in the area near his cave and starts schools for the children who begin entering his communities. He shepherds these monasteries for over two decades.

c. 525. Boëthius is accused of conspiracy with the Byzantine Empire, and is executed by Theodoric.

526. Theodoric dies. His death destabilizes Italy, opening the region to more invasions.

527. Justinian I becomes emperor of the Eastern Roman Empire.

c. 529. The jealous priest Florentius works to undermine the discipline at Benedict's monasteries in Subiaco, so Benedict moves his monks to Monte Cassino.

c. 530. After a long foreground of contemplation and revision, Benedict writes down his *Rule.* He also revises it over the years. It will become the foundation of Western monasticism and also a spiritual classic for laypeople. Sometime during his Monte Cassino experience, Benedict founds a monastery on the coast near Tarracina.

535. Emperor Justinian commands General Belisarius to invade Italy.

540. Gregory (the Great) is born. He later becomes St. Benedict's first biographer.

542. At Monte Cassino, Benedict is visited by the Goth King Totila, probably late in the year, when Totila is marching through the area on his way to attack Naples. This meeting is the only fairly certain date we have for Benedict.

547. Scholastica comes to visit Benedict one last time. Three days later, she dies. Benedict has his shining vision of God and of the whole world. Not long after the death of his sister, he dies at Monte Cassino, while standing in prayer.

21 March 547. This is the traditional date set for Benedict's death. This date is somewhat supported by Gregory's account of a visit to Benedict from Sabinus, the bishop of Canusium, during which the bishop mentioned Totila's imminent destruction of Rome. Some historians have taken this reference to mean Totila's brief occupation of the imperial city that began on December 17th, 546. (In the spring of 547, the city was recaptured by Belisarius.)

549. King Totila captures Rome, as Benedict had prophesied.

c. 550. This rounded date is often given for Benedict's death. Between 546 and 550 seems the most likely window for Benedict's death.

July 552. King Totila dies in the battle of Taginae, ending the long, cruel conflicts between the Ostrogothic Kingdom in Italy and the Roman Byzantine Empire. This victory fulfills Justinian's dream of ruling a reunited Eastern and Western Roman Empire.

565. Emperor Justinian I dies.

568. Close on the heels of the defeated Ostrogoths, the ruthless Germanic Lombards invade northern Italy under King Alboin, infamous for fashioning a drinking-cup out of the skull of his defeated enemy, King Cunimund. The Lombards—"that abominable people," according to Gregory—rule until 774.

573. Gregory is appointed Prefect of the city of Rome *(Praefectus Urbi)*.

575. Gregory becomes a Benedictine monk and wants to be a missionary.

c. 581. The Monte Cassino monastery is destroyed by the Lombards (as Benedict prophesied), and the monks flee to Rome, carrying a copy of Benedict's *Rule* and other spiritual treasures. The Lombards also destroy the Subiaco and Tarracina monasteries.

590. Gregory is made pope (reluctantly). The eighth-century church historian and Benedictine monk the Venerable Bede, in his *Historia Ecclesiastica Gentis Anglorum (Ecclesiastical History of the English People)* calls the new pope "a distinguished scholar and administrator." Gregory is hesitant to become pope, however, because he does not want to leave the rich spiritual monastic life for the administrative and other pressures of the papacy. In fact, he opens the first book of his *Dialogues* with this complaint to his deacon Peter:

> My unhappy soul languish[es] under a burden of distractions. I recall those earlier days in the monastery where I could rise above the vanities of life. But now all the beauty

of that spiritual repose is gone, and the contact with worldly men and their affairs, which is a necessary part of my duties as bishop, has left my soul defiled. I am tossed about on the waves of a heavy sea, and my soul is like a helpless ship buffeted by raging winds.[1]

593. Pope Gregory writes the four books of his *Dialogues*. Book Two contains the only contemporary account of Benedict's life, released within fifty years of his death.

597. This year, as Bede records in his *Ecclesiastical History*, Pope Gregory is "inspired by God to send his servant Augustine [*not* St. Augustine the Great of Hippo] with several other God-fearing monks to preach God's word to the English nation." But they quickly grow afraid and want to return home, so they send Augustine back to Gregory to let him know the trip is too dangerous. They want to be ordered back to Rome. Gregory's answer sums up his theology:

> Be faithful and enthusiastic in carrying out this mission. Remember that the greater the labor, the greater the glory of your eternal reward. When your leader Augustine returns, obey him in everything, humbly, and know that whatever he asks you to do, will always be for the good of your souls.[2]

Early in the 700s. Pope Gregory II commissions the rebuilding of the Monte Cassino monastery.

15 February 1944. Allied forces bomb the monastery at Monte Cassino into rubble. Two months earlier, the German Army had had fifteen divisions entrenched on the hill, complete with concrete bunkers, turreted machine guns, barbed wire, and minefields, and the Allied forces had taken heavy losses trying to win Monte Cassino. When

the U.S. Army had exhausted its strength by February 1944, it was replaced by the New Zealand Corps, and the order was given to bomb the monastery, even though the Allied soldiers in the trenches asserted repeatedly that no German fire had come from the monastery. But the bombing command stood. After the U.S. Air Force obliterated Monte Cassino, the rubble itself became an excellent defensive position for the German Army. From it, ironically, the German soldiers could better defend the hill. Several more failed attacks were made on Monte Cassino after the bombing, and this strategic hill was not taken by Allied forces until the eighteenth of May 1944.

1950s. The monastery at Monte Cassino is rebuilt with international funds.

24 October 1964. Pope Paul VI visits Monte Cassino to proclaim St. Benedict the patron saint of Europe. St. Benedict is named "Messenger of Peace, Unifier, Master of Civilization, Herald of Faith, and Initiator of Monastic Life in Western Europe."

11 July. St. Benedict's feast day is celebrated yearly. Patron saint of monks, farmers, schoolchildren, spelunkers, and land reclamation, he is also the patron saint of Europe.

MAN OF BLESSING

CHAPTER 1

MEDIEVAL BIOGRAPHY

The only ancient account of Benedict is found in the second volume of Pope Gregory the Great's four-book *Dialogues,* written in 593. Book Two consists of a prologue and thirty-eight succinct chapters. The noted nineteenth-century Roman historian Thomas Hodgkin praised St. Gregory's life of St. Benedict as "the biography of the greatest monk, written by the greatest Pope, himself also a monk."[5]

Gregory's account of this saint's life is not, however, a biography in the modern sense of the word. It provides instead a genuine spiritual portrait of the gentle, disciplined Abbot.

In a letter to Bishop Maximilian of Syracuse, Gregory states his intention for his *Dialogues,* saying they are a kind of *floretum (anthology,* literally, "flowers") of the most striking miracles of Italian holy men.[6] Gregory did not therefore set out to write a chronological, historically anchored story of Benedict, as our twenty-first-century minds might expect, but he was conscientious in basing his stories of this saint on direct testimony. To establish his authority, Gregory explains that his information came from the best sources, a handful of Benedict's disciples who lived with the saint and witnessed his various miracles. These followers, he says, are Constantinus, who succeeded Benedict as abbot of Monte Cassino; Valentinianus; Simplicius; and Honoratus, who was abbot of Subiaco when Gregory wrote his *Dialogues*.

In Gregory's day, history was not recognized as an independent field of study; it was a branch of grammar or rhetoric, and *historia* (defined as "story") summed up the approach of learned persons when they wrote what was at that time considered "history."[7] Gregory's *Dialogues* Book Two, then, as an authentic medieval hagiography cast as a conversation between the pope and his deacon Peter, is designed to teach spiritual lessons. It still does, for these wise stories are as relevant in the third millennium as they were in the first.

Gregory knew the seminal hagiography, *The Life of Saint Anthony*, written by St. Athanasius. This *Life* set the standard by which all later works of the genre were judged, and all saints' lives incorporated common elements. Born to wealthy parents, St. Anthony gave up his inheritance and went out into the Egyptian desert, as Benedict fled Rome's worldliness for the wilderness of Subiaco. From St. Anthony's third-century, northern-Egyptian, semi-eremetical monasticism (and from Pachomius' coenobitical monks in south Egypt), Christian monasticism first developed, and from Benedict's solitude, Western monasticism was likewise born.

Although medieval hagiography by its very nature had to include deserts, wildernesses, hermithood, and miracles, it is difficult to pinpoint Gregory's precise attitude toward the last of these. In the first book of *Dialogues,* when a doubting Peter admits, "I don't know of any Italians whose lives give evidence of extraordinary spiritual powers," the pope replies that if he were to describe all the miracles he himself knows that have been accomplished by saints, he would run out of time before he would run out of wonders. To Gregory, miracles are events by which God catches our attention, wakes us from spiritual laziness, and teaches us about His holy nature.[8] Moses' turning aside to see the burning bush is a good example. That is why Gregory felt the Church especially needed miracles in times of tribulation, to rouse it from despair and to sustain it.

In a letter to St. Augustine of Canterbury, Gregory verbalizes his acceptance of miracles as natural events performed by those who are holy, but he gives a strong warning concerning their performance, as the Venerable Bede records:

> My dearest brother, I hear Almighty God worked great miracles through you for His chosen English nation. Now let me say about these divine gifts, that they are from God, and you should feel a respectful joy for them, and a joyful respect. Be joyful that the souls of the English are attracted through these visible, exterior miracles to an inner grace, but never lose your hunger for humility, or your fragile mind might become proud applauding itself for these wonderful events.[9]

Here Gregory's restraint toward miracles is remarkable for the light it sheds on his pastoral approach. He readily acknowledges the awe-inspiring power of wonders to spark a person's belief, but he does not want anyone falling into an unhealthy fascination with these external manifestations of faith—he wants them to rely instead on an inner, day-by-day preoccupation with and cultivation of God's love within their souls.

Most medieval believers would have viewed the miracles attributed to Benedict as the power a saint is expected and even assumed to have over nature and other humans. Sophisticated medieval readers—monks, nuns, and the ordained of the Church—would have believed in miracles, too, but might have focused primarily on their symbolic significance. Most significantly, the people and places associated with Benedict's miracles did exist and do tell us much about him as a person.

As Gregory intended, the miracles showcase the pastoral nature of Abbot Benedict's ministry, demonstrating how Benedict helped others achieve peace in the minutiae of ordinary life. Book Two of *Dialogues* includes thirty-six of these stories. One shows Benedict coming to the aid of a monk who lost some monastic property. Gregory tells how one of Benedict's monks lost the blade of a scythe while clearing a thorn-infested area for a garden. He had been working all morning beside a large lake when the blade loosened and slipped from his scythe as he swung it, landing with a disheartening plop far out in the water, gone.

The brother was upset. Tools were precious. He knew Benedict's *Rule* cultivates a proper respect for them, as it advises in chapter thirty-two, "If anyone handles the monastery's property disrespectfully or carelessly, they should be corrected." Also, this monk was a Goth, an outsider, and, before coming to Abbot Benedict's monastery, he might have been bullied as a pagan soldier by a superior officer in a marauding Gothic army, or he might have lived the life of a browbeaten servant, receiving regular doses of harsh physical treatment and abusive words. His panic at losing the tool might also suggest he was accustomed to being berated when things went wrong, whether or not he was to blame.

When Benedict was notified of this problem, he did not send a messenger, but went himself and told the monk not to worry. Benedict picked up the naked scythe handle and stuck it in the shallow water at the lake's edge. The Goth relaxed in the Abbot's comforting presence, happy in the dawning realization that he was, in fact, not in trouble for losing a valuable tool. Resting his hands on his knees, he bent beside Benedict, his face turned to study the curious movements of his Abbot. But his relief turned to amazement as he saw the blade pop up through the wet surface. It had risen from the soft mud bottom some distance out. He watched it glide through the dark lake water to meet the handle, then reattach itself.

CHAPTER 2

GREGORY AND BENEDICT

Gregory presents the miracle of the scythe as an extension of the Abbot's kindness; therefore, this story is best understood when read side-by-side with Gregory's most well-known work, the *Liber pastoralis curae,* or *Pastoral Care,* composed soon after he became pope in 590, which was only a few years before he wrote the life of Benedict in 593. In *Pastoral Care,* Gregory outlines the duties of those who serve the Church. He says they must especially guard against putting their own ambitions and ego before God.

In *Pastoral Care,* Gregory also stresses that the clergy must know the individuals in their congregations well and must serve each of them compassionately and humbly. A clergyman must be "a neighbor in compassion to everyone and exalted above all in thought, so that by the love of his heart he may transfer to himself the infirmities of others."[10] A close examination of this influential Gregorian text highlights the many ways Gregory presents Benedict's life as the fulfillment of all he has outlined in *Pastoral Care.* In his *Dialogues,* Gregory's main theme is that Benedict was not someone who sent others to do his pastoral work. He went himself.

The musical image introducing Part III of Gregory's *Pastoral Care* outlines the sensitivity required of those who minister:

> The discourse of a teacher should be adapted to the character of the hearers, so as to be suited to the individual in his respective needs, and yet never deviate from the art of general edification. For what else are the minds of attentive hearers but, if I may say so, the taut strings of a harp, which the skillful harpist plays with a variety of strokes, that he may not produce a discordant melody? And it is for this reason that the strings give forth a harmonious melody, because they are not plucked with the same kind of stroke, though plucked with the one plectrum. Hence, too, every teacher, in order to edify all in the one virtue of charity, must touch the hearts of his hearers by using one and the same doctrine, but not by giving to all one and the same exhortation. [11]

Next, Gregory lists page after careful page of gender, age, and psychological differences that must be identified and understood in an audience, if the minister is to give wise counsel. He must distinguish between

> men and women; the young and the old; the poor and the rich; the joyful and the sad; subjects and superiors; slaves and masters; the wise of this world and the dull; the impudent and the timid; the insolent and the faint-hearted; the impatient and the patient; the kindly and

the envious; the sincere and the insincere; the hale and the sick; those who fear afflictions and, therefore, live innocently, and those so hardened in evil as to be impervious to the correction of affliction; the taciturn and the loquacious; the slothful and the hasty; the meek and the choleric; the humble and the haughty; the obstinate and the fickle; the gluttonous and the abstemious; those who mercifully give of their own, and those addicted to thieving. . . .[12]

This exceedingly detailed (i.e., very Gregorian) enumeration runs on for one-and-a-half more pages, and subsequent chapters give explicit instructions on how to communicate uniquely sensitive guidance to each of these individuals.

Gregory's focus on pastoral work is also evident in the most famous sequence of puns in English historical writing. Purportedly made by the pope about the early English (of the "Angles" tribe), and recorded by Bede in his *Ecclesiastical History,* as well as in *The Earliest Life of Gregory the Great by an Anonymous Monk of Whitby,*[13] this trinity of paronomasia is emblematic of Gregory's pastoral heart.

Bede says the pope was passing by a Roman slave market when he spied a group of Angle children being sold as slaves. Their stunning fair skin and blue eyes slowed him, and he asked where they were from. When Gregory learned the children were Angles, he replied, "Not Angles, *angels.*" Then he asked the name of their king, and when he was told, "Alle," he countered with, "Alleluia! God's praise must be heard in His kingdom." Finally, when he inquired after the name of their region and was told, "Deira" (in modern-day Yorkshire), he was said to have retorted, "But they will flee from the anger [*de ira*] of God to the faith." At a time when Pope Gregory was besieged at home in Rome by famine and civil unrest, and hampered in his own body by chronic pain, he still looked outward, became aware of a need in England, and sent St. Augustine there.

Also, books one, three, and four of the *Dialogues* present the lives of other Italian abbots and bishops as patterns of the holy lifestyle fellow Christians would do well to follow. Gregory reminds his readers that these miracles represent the power of Christian virtues, which are available to all. The fourth book particularly discusses eschatological matters, to show the spiritual efficacy of masses and good deeds. Gregory gives eyewitness accounts of the world beyond this one, including the punishments awaiting unrepentant souls. He reminds Peter, "These visions of hell are useful as warnings, turning many from evil," and, "It is better to die and exit this life a free person, than to look for liberty after you find yourself in the chains of the afterlife."

Throughout his *Dialogues,* Gregory seems mindful of the opening statement of St. Athanasius' *Life of Saint Anthony:* "I know you will hear and marvel at the life of this saint, and that you will also want to follow in his footsteps, for Anthony's days show monks how to live the ascetic way." In other words, Gregory wrote his four-volume collection, devoting one book to Benedict's life, to bolster the faith of

Christians living in a post-Roman Empire world of plague, famine, drought, pagan invasions, and ecclesiastical schism. His thesis is that God is still in control, despite outward signs of conflict—that the age of great saints, miracles, and hope is not over. He seems to be reminding himself of this truth, as much as anyone else. In our own age of instability, violence, terrorism, epidemics, famine, drought, ecclesiastical angst, and divisive politics, Gregory's vivid account of the life of the peaceful monk Benedict speaks to us all.

CHAPTER 3

A GOLDEN ROMAN

The baby who would grow up to be St. Benedict was born around 480 in a tiny hill village in Umbria. This area's name originated with the sixth-century BC Italic tribe known as *the Umbri*. A written record of their religious rituals was discovered in 1444 in Gubbio, with the unearthing of the seven bronze Iguvine Tablets, a major archaeological find. These tablets revealed secret rites (in both Etruscan and in Latin) practiced by the Umbri's pagan priesthood, called the *Fratres Arvales* (or Arval Brethren, from *arvus*, for "plowed field"). This sacred brotherhood dated back to the third century BC, and its patrician members would probably have been active during the first three centuries AD (from Emperor Augustus through Emperor Theodosius I).

As its sacrificial victim was paraded around a cornfield, the entire farming community danced, sang praises to the corn deity, Dea Dia (a relative of Ceres), and presented her with offerings of wine, milk, and honey. These were also aimed at placating the dreaded Mars, or god of blight. The rituals of these early fertility-god worshipers read like a page from Shirley Jackson's chilling short story, "The Lottery," and this vestigial pagan devotion was to be an obstacle Benedict would face later in his ministry.

The astonishing beauty of Benedict's birthplace—"Bella Umbria"—is glimpsed in the Renaissance paintings of the Umbrian artist known simply as Perugino, well known today as Raphael's teacher. In works like *St. Jerome in the Wilderness, The Baptism of Jesus,* and *The Combat of Love and Chastity,* the region's stark mountains, snow-water lakes, and gently rolling green hills frame holy moments and divine struggles, as they must have done for Benedict.

In reality, some of these peaks reach 8,000-plus feet (2,438 meters) and are the heart of the Apennines mountain range, that backbone of the Italian peninsula. Like Tuscany, its more famous neighbor to the northwest, Umbria has always been overrun with fecund olive groves, vineyards, cypress woods, lavender bushes, cherry orchards, and mulberry trees, and, in these, the twelfth-century Umbrian St. Francis of Assisi always found beautiful, singing birds:

> There certainly seems to have been a divine prophecy both in the joy of the different kinds of birds and in the song of the falcon—a prophecy of the time when this praiser and worshiper of God would be lifted up on the wings of contemplation and there would be exalted with a Seraphic vision.[14]

This area also inspired St. Francis's "Brother Sun" song, praising God for every creature, including Brother Sun, Sister Moon and the stars, Brother Wind, Sister Water,

Brother Fire, and the sustaining Sister Earth who produces all the different kinds of fruits, brightly colored flowers, and green plants.

And, earlier, in *The Georgics,* the exiled Virgil celebrated Umbria's "abundant fruit and wine," "fat herds and olives," "sacred streams," "crystal lakes," and land "rich with silver, copper, and gold." He also sang of its natural rigors, and especially its bitter-cold winters, calling this mountain district "frigid Nursia" and its Apennine heights "rocky" and "harsh," and saying its "thin soil" bred mountaineers who "excelled in toughness."

Benedict was one of these.

CHAPTER 4

IN A DARK TIME

Fifth-century Italy was not, however, an auspicious time to be born. Benedict's home was a war-torn, disease-and-hunger-plagued land. Its future was inexorably linked to the fate of a collapsing Roman Empire, and *uncertainty* was the watchword of the day. The once-unstoppable Roman Empire had disintegrated against barbarian invasions, a weak economy, and its own civil wars. The Goth Alaric invaded first in 400, followed by Attila the Hun in mid-century and Geiseric the King of the Vandals. These foreigners—blind to everything but victory at any cost—pillaged their way through the peninsula's enchanting landscape.

When in 476 the Germanic chieftain (and former Roman mercenary) Odoacer overthrew the boy-emperor Romulus Augustus, the Western Roman Empire was effectively ended, as the first-century historian Tacitus might have said, by an upstart barbarian and his Teutonic soldiers—an infantry of men as strong as their ancestors, and with the same "fierce blue eyes and huge frames." Odoacer made himself the *dux* of Italy, but relations between this Hun-Scirian and the

Eastern Roman Empire soured; in 489 the Eastern Roman Emperor Zeno invited the Goth (and Arian) Theodoric the Great to invade Italy.

For three years, battles raged. Theodoric and his army conquered in the Isonzo Valley and at Milan, and they took territory along the Adda River up north. In February of 493, they besieged and captured Odoacer's Ravenna, the old Western Roman capital. This victory established Theodoric as King of the Ostrogoths in Italy. The peninsula was his.

When the vanquished Germanic chieftain Odoacer surrendered and agreed to a power-sharing treaty, Theodoric summoned him and his son to a "celebratory" banquet, only to murder them there. Despite this fatal start, Theodoric had a long, successful reign (493–526). The four decades of his power coincided with Benedict's adulthood, and the modicum of stability they provided proved beneficial to this saint and his work. As king, Theodoric respected Roman laws and institutions, repaired Italy's infrastructure of Roman roads, harbors, and public buildings, and defended Italy against the Franks.

In a letter to Unigis, Theodoric's secretary, Cassiodorus, records the benign policies of this pagan king:

> We are pleased to live under the law of the Romans and to defend them with our armies, and we are just as interested in maintaining morality as we are in warring successfully; for what good would it do to eradicate barbarian riots, if we didn't then live lawfully? Let other kings chase the glory of battle and conquered cities. Our purpose is, *Deo volente*, to rule so well that

our subjects will regret they did not know the blessings of our reign much earlier.[15]

Theodoric's achievements as a ruler led medieval chroniclers to regard him as an "atypical pagan," but during his tenure, Rome's standing in the world slipped further. It became a backwater, and even King Theodoric made only one trip during his entire long reign from Ravenna across the Apennines and down to Rome.

When Theodoric died in 526, invaders redoubled their efforts until, nearly a decade later in 535, Eastern Roman Emperor Justinian I invaded Italy with his legions, commanded by the canny General Belisarius. Benedict was then likely a fifty-something monk. Fresh from victories in North Africa, Justinian wanted to take Italy from the Ostrogoths so he could be crowned emperor of a reunited Western and Eastern Roman Empire.

Justinian's ambition caused Italians decades of suffering. Single Umbrian mothers increased, and they had the task of feeding their fatherless children in a time of famine. Tacitus describes this painful impulse well: "Lust for power is ancient and ingrained in the human soul." Justinian's obsession brought him into armed conflict for years with the Ostrogothic King Baduila *(nom de guerre,* Totila), who himself wanted to restore the Ostrogothic kingdom in Italy. Totila did take Rome in 549, but he died three years later in the battle of Taginae, ending the long, bloody wars on the peninsula between the Ostrogothic Kingdom and the Roman Byzantine Empire. Emperor Justinian had gained his evanescent crown.

Although Justinian was known for his judicial reforms, perhaps his more-lasting (and least-flattering) portrait was drafted by the Roman historian Procopius, who traveled with Belisarius on the eastern front. In his much-debated *Secret History,* Procopius maligns Justinian:

> He was simultaneously evil and agreeable. To put it colloquially, he was a moron. He never spoke the truth. He was always mendacious in what he said and did, but he was also easily tricked by anyone wanting to deceive him. His personality was a perverse mix of idiocy and cruelty. Without hesitation, he ordered the raping of countries, the sacking of cities, and the wholesale enslavement of nations, for no reason. If you cared to add up every tragedy that happened to the Romans before Justinian came to power, and then compared these with this emperor's list of heinous crimes, I think you would quickly discover that more people were murdered by this one man than in all of history.[16]

Generations, then, of man-made trauma, the dissolution of society, and the disruption of community were the backdrop for Benedict's *Rule,* and they contrasted greatly with its main theme—peace with God and harmony with others. Perhaps the constant warring and myopic greed of Benedict's age made him gravitate to and stick with this message of *pax.*

CHAPTER 5

FAMILY AND EDUCATION

enedict learned the importance of family at an early age. Growing up in a Roman family, he was taught that the most sacred institution is family and that the father (or *paterfamilias*) is its respected leader. His word was law. The other guiding principle of Benedict's earliest years was a Roman reverence for obedience to a larger, worthy cause.

Although these cultural standards were tested and even modified in the years to come by Benedict's growing Christian faith, both of these essentially Roman values are written indelibly into his *Rule*. For example, Benedict outlines in chapters two and sixty-four that the abbot "must show the tough attitude of a master, and also the loving affection of a father," and "he ought, therefore, to be learned in the divine law, so that he may know it well, and that it may be for him a store whence he draws forth new things and old, as seems best in each case."[17] The monks' submission to what is best for the community, rather than to what is most attractive for each one of them personally, is meant to be accomplished by their holy obedience to the

Christ-like abbot, "without fearfulness, without slowness in performance, without half-heartedness or grumbling or an unwilling reply."[18]

Tradition also gives Benedict a twin sister, Scholastica ("learned"). We have no historical proof of her existence, but this convention was sanctioned by the ancient historian Bede. As a child, Scholastica was dedicated to God, suggesting Benedict's family was Christian. Custom also teaches that she served later as the superior of convents under Benedict's abbacy at Subiaco and in Plumbariola, several miles from Monte Cassino, but this cannot be determined with certainty. Other historians believe Scholastica may have in fact lived at the base of Monte Cassino in a hermitage (or *vicus),* with one or two other religious women, because there is an ancient church named after her. To Gregory's mind, Scholastica is most significant for the intimate relationship that she and her brother shared, centered in their mutual service to God.

Around the time St. Patrick died in Ireland in 493, Benedict moved from his birthplace in Nursia some hundred miles southwest to Rome. The shift from rural Nursia to the more sophisticated city of Rome, with its impressive, "imperial" buildings and culture, was probably a dramatic one for the teenaged Benedict. Here he lived a privileged life with his family and nurse, and began to study in Rome's classical schools.

The Roman educational system consisted first of home schooling, and then of elementary school, grammar school, and the school of rhetoric. Benedict's first teachers were his parents. At home or later in elementary school, Benedict was taught the rudimentaries of reading, writing, and arithmetic. A *litterator* or *magister litterarius* would have taught him how to use a wax tablet and a pointed steel stylus for writing. When young Benedict had learned this basic technology, he advanced to writing on the more expensive papyrus.

Next came grammar school. Students reported before dawn to begin learning. Here their reading broadened to include Latin and Greek literature, especially the poetry of Virgil, Horace, Ovid, and Homer, which they were taught by the more advanced teacher, the *grammaticus*. Roman youth like Benedict studied the pastoral tradition in Virgil, who writes, for example, a long poem praising the humble bee, making "the manna, the heavenly gift of honey," and they encountered the *carpe diem* work of Horace, who encourages indulgence:

> Drink free! . . .
> Tomorrow and her works defy;
> Lay hold upon the present hour,
> And snatch the pleasures passing by,
> To put them out of Fortune's power.[19]

Horace specifically defines for young men the transient worldly pleasures they should enjoy:

> The appointed hour of promised bliss,
> The pleasing whisper in the dark,
> The half-unwilling, willing kiss,
> The laugh that guides thee to the mark.[20]

Benedict also likely read Ovid's stories of classical mythology and of the world's creation:

> Stars, like brilliant bubbles, rose and shone;
> Birds beat the air, the beasts had earth to roam,
> And flickering fish in water found a home.
> There wanted yet, to dominate the whole,
> A more capacious mind, a loftier soul;
> So man was formed of elements conveyed
> Direct from heaven, some think, by him who made
> Order prevail in chaos—him I call
> The cosmic architect, who fashioned all.[21]

Gymnastics was also part of the Roman grammar school curriculum. This training included wrestling, running, jumping, and other sports considered track-and-field events today. These were intended to strengthen the students' bodies for future hardships, particularly on global battlefields. Providentially, however, this early athletic training tempered this singular Roman youth for God, equipping Benedict for the strenuous and rather unexpected career of hermithood. His young body was being toughened to abandon all comforts of home and submit to the unforgiving wilderness with its often punishing weather. His grammar school physical education training was preparing him to fight the invisible wars of the soul.

CHAPTER 6

SCHOOL OF RHETORIC

Then, at seventeen, Benedict gave up his boyhood tunic for a Roman toga and enrolled in a school of rhetoric. The emphasis of his studies shifted. He read and analyzed classical prose and also practiced and eventually mastered (as witnessed by his *Rule*) the skills of composition and public speaking, under the tutelage of a *rhetor*. Benedict must have spent hours studying the plays, speeches, letters, and philosophical epigrams of Seneca and Cicero.

He might, for example, have read Seneca's Stoic description of death, with its dismissal of heaven and hell:

> After death nothing is, and nothing death:
> The utmost limits of a gasp of breath.
> Let the ambitious zealot lay aside his hopes of heaven;
> whose faith is but his pride.
> Let slavish souls lay by their feat,
> Nor be concerned which way or where
> After this life they shall be hurled;
> Dead, we become the lumber of the world,
> And to that mass of matter shall be swept

Where things destroyed with things unborn are kept:
Devouring time swallows us whole,
Impartial death confounds body and soul.
For Hell, and the foul Fiend that rules
The everlasting fiery jails,
Devised by rogues, dreaded by fools,
With his grim grisly dog that keeps the door,
Are senseless stories, idle tales,
Dreams, whimsies, and no more.[22]

But young Benedict had an old soul. He was disturbed by the misuse and triviality of "rhetoric for rhetoric's sake," something persisting today as *advertising,* and *politics.* In a similar fashion, St. Augustine said in Book Eight of *Confessions* he found in the Word of God that which he could not find in his rhetoric textbooks, those "tedious . . . trifles of trifles and vanities of vanities" (Chapters VI, XI).

In *Institutiones Divinarum et Sæcularium Litterarum (Introduction to Divine and Human Readings),* Cassiodorus presents a clear picture of this shallowness:

When I saw secular studies being pursued with great fervor, so much so that a great mass of men believed such studies would bring them the wisdom of this world, I confess I was seriously perturbed that there should be no public professors of Holy Scripture, when worldly texts were the beneficiaries of a distinguished educational tradition.[23]

Benedict might also have read (and disagreed with) Ur-orator Cicero's words on brevity: "Brevity, in fact—on some occasions—is a real excellence, but it is also far from being compatible with the general character of what I would call eloquence."[24] Benedict's later decisions would demonstrate that this former student of rhetoric believed learning to say the expected thing in the proper, most persuasive way was not as valuable to him as learning to walk along the Way of truth and listen to the *Logos*. A knowledge of Benedict's early training in Roman rhetoric adds heft and definition to his writing, for he teaches in chapter twenty of his *Rule* that communal prayer must not be long-winded and pompous, but "brief and sincere."

During these years in the Roman schools, Benedict might have met Eastern monastic movement leaders and might have also begun reading the monastic rules circulating around. He could have pored over St. Basil's fourth-century *Rule,* which presents wisdom still followed today by Greek Orthodox and Catholic monastics. St. Basil believed the foundation of all asceticism is a dedicated submission to the authority of the Holy Scriptures, to the extent that he apologized for having to use extra-Biblical words in his writings[25]. St. Benedict followed St. Basil in this Biblical emphasis, salting his short *Rule* with abundant scriptural references, including the parable from Jesus that recommends listening to God's word: "Everyone then who hears these words of mine and acts on them will be like a wise man who built his house on rock" (Matthew 7:24). St. Basil also stresses in his *Rule* that the dialogue of community nurtures the individual: "In this communal conversation, whatever is twisted in us will be straightened and whatever is good will be strengthened, and it will help us avoid being condemned with those who are only wise in their own eyes."[26]

Benedict might have also read the *Rule* composed by the Doctor of Grace, with its emphasis on fraternal bonds. St. Augustine's message of community is summed up in the title for the first chapter: "The Basic Belief: Mutual Love Expressed in the Community of Goods and in Humility"; he opens with this instruction: "Above all things, *live together in harmony, being of one mind and one heart* (Acts 4:32) as you walk God's way. Isn't this the exact reason you came to live together?"[27]

As Benedict sat in a Roman classroom, he read a wide variety of liberal arts texts, and the direction of his adult life took shape. He was a teenager discovering he had little in common with his classmates, who were mostly interested in repeating a dull cycle of studying and drunken partying. Rome's political and moral corruption also bothered Benedict.

The Roman habit of a three-course dinner *(cena)* for the upper class would have been irresistible to most elite students, mainly for the abundant wine served (customarily watered-down and fortified with honey). Drinking the Falernian white wine Horace sings of in his *Odes,* often from priapic-shaped cups, the young men lounged on couches and also ate delicacies like roasted peacock, then stuffed figs for dessert, while they watched the dancing girls, and each other.

Horace writes that the feasters ate "like wild pigs, gulping loud," and Juvenal also describes these young Romans in his *Third Satire:*

They praise the burping and long-pissing Lords,
and nothing's sacred or free
from their unceasing ungodly lechery.[28]

Benedict would have been expected to leverage his social position and wealth. Destined to contribute to society in law or politics, he would have likely found himself in the process of choosing a life-path far different from the one he had been born to inherit, and he must have felt the pressure of his heritage. He might have experienced sharp loneliness as his character diverged from that of his contemporaries. Maybe he read with poignancy Cicero's letter to his friend Atticus in northwestern Greece:

I must say, there is nothing I miss so much at the moment as a man with whom I can share all my worries, who is fond of me and sensible, to whom I can speak without any pretense or reserve or concealment. My spectacular friendships with the great, though they are not without glamour in the big world, give me no enjoyment in private. So when my house is well filled with callers in the morning, and I go down to the Forum surrounded with troops of friends, I cannot find in all that crowd a single soul with whom I can exchange either an unguarded joke or an intimate grumble.[29]

Perhaps Benedict broke off his rigorous classical studies from time to time to contemplate this telling verse from the fifteenth chapter of the Gospel of John: "If you belonged to the world, the world would love you as its own. Because you do not belong to the world, but I have chosen you out of the world—therefore the world hates you."[30]

CHAPTER 7

DISINHERITANCE AND A CRACKED SIFTER

round the year 500, as a new century dawned, Benedict left Rome. Repelled by the compromised lives of his so-called "well-educated" companions, he went in search of a new context. Quitting school, he abandoned home, wealth, inheritance, worldly status, and the potential comforts of a wife, choosing God instead. His "only desire," Gregory said, was "to please the Lord" (*"soli Deo placere cupiens"*).

Juvenal describes with pointed satire the evils of Rome rejected by Benedict—mendacity, astrology, patricide, divination, illicit love, and political corruption:

> What should I do at Rome? I have not learnt
> The art of lying. If a book be bad,
> I cannot praise and ask to take it home.
> I am ignorant of the movements of the stars.
> I neither will nor can promise a son
> His father's death. The entrails of a frog
> Never did I inspect. Others possess

More skill than I to convey to a wife
Presents and messages from a paramour.
From me no thief can expect aid; and so
No Governor will appoint me to his staff.[31]

We can only speculate what Benedict's family thought of this spectacular U-turn in his life. Because Gregory is remarkably silent about Benedict's parents, the words of Jesus to His disciples come to mind: "[E]veryone who has left houses or brothers or sisters or father or mother or children or fields, for my name's sake, will receive a hundredfold, and will inherit eternal life" (Matthew 19:29).

Whatever the situation at home in Nursia, Benedict's old nurse remained by his side. When he headed for Enfide (the contemporary Affile), she faithfully accompanied him. This move took them some forty miles east into the Simbrucini Mountains. It would not have been a particularly easy journey for the no-longer-young woman. At a slow pace, this distance required at least two days of hard walking. Perhaps Benedict stopped after forty miles because he decided he had to find a new home before his nurse's health was compromised.

Benedict and his loyal servant initially settled near a church dedicated to St. Peter. The Christian community there put them up in travelers' lodging. Meeting some men who shared his moral and spiritual concerns, Benedict established community with them. He was firmly on a new path.

Young Benedict also worked his first miracle in Enfide. When his nurse borrowed a clay *capisterium,* a valuable kitchen sifter used for winnowing wheat, she accidentally left it on a table, and it was knocked on the floor and broke completely in half. She was deeply upset over this accident, especially since she had borrowed the sieve from their new neighbors and did not know how she could replace it.

As the son of wealth, Benedict could have reprimanded his servant for making a fuss over a trifle. But when he saw her crying about the cracked sieve, her worry became his own. Gregory used this first miracle to show Benedict's compassion in the little things of life. Gregory taught that God is in the quotidian, those easily overlooked spaces where *compassion* also gathers meaning. *Passion* originates in the root *pati,* for "to suffer," so *com*-passion literally signifies "to suffer *with.*" Gregory's telling of the miracle of the sieve demonstrates that no matter how universal suffering is, it always happens in the familiar specific.

In the retelling below of the miracle of the sieve, this twenty-first-century biographer of Benedict attempts to follow Gregory's wise lead by casting her stories of this Italian abbot into dialogue—not between Gregory and Peter—but between Benedict and his neighbors. Gregory's innovative use of dialogue between the personae of himself as pope and his deacon Peter dramatically frames the stories he tells of Benedict, allowing the audience to fully participate in the spiritual wisdom of these stories.[32] As a scholar of the Church, Gregory also knew the profound etymology of *dialogue, dia-*("across") plus the *Logos* of John 1:1, meaning literally, "to speak a word across [or alternately]."

Another reason I have chosen to ground the life of this saint in conversations is that his whole life centered on an understanding that God's *Logos* was synonymous with his name, *Benedict*: "the well-spoken or well-said word." This moniker, in turn, reminds us of the true nature of *conversation* (literally, "to turn," *vert-*, "with or together," *com-*, or "to turn toward [someone]"). Turning to God's word, and listening to it, we are then meant to turn toward each other with good words and deeds. This godly lifestyle is capsulized in the shared linguistic roots of *convert* and *conversation*, which suggest the most active type of listening possible, a listening that is one with doing. The wisdom of hearing Holy Scripture and loving in a community is the foundation of Benedict's ministry, because he believed that the Bible contains the words of the Word that makes all words of true communication possible.

So what did young Benedict do when his nurse broke that clay sieve? He picked up the pieces and went to his room, where he turned to God in prayer. He prayed a long time. When he stopped and looked at the kitchen tool, it was no longer broken. Astonished, he twisted it upside down in his hands and examined its bottom, saw no indication the sieve had ever been anything but whole—no splits, no ridges, no tell-tale scars were visible. It was entirely smooth, exactly as it was before it fell off the table. Holding the restored sieve in two hands, he rushed to his nurse.

"It's fixed! Look! You can't tell it broke! Don't worry now. It's good as new! Here!"

His nurse took the sifter in her unsteady hands and walked off to tell the neighbors. Before long, everyone had heard of this miracle. The people in the village hung the restored sieve above the church door, reminding everyone present and also future generations of Benedict's miracle. They viewed this as the first sign that God was blessing with miraculous power Benedict's renunciation of the world, and so that common household implement hung above the door of this ordinary church for years to come. Possibly it was hanging there, mute, when the rowdy, pagan Lombards rode through Enfide toward the end of that same century, destroying everything fragile in their way.

CHAPTER 8

UNWANTED CELEBRITY

This miraculous event brought Benedict unlooked-for local fame. He escaped it by leaving Enfide, and his nurse there, and hiking two-and-a-half miles north to Subiaco. En route he met Romanus, a monk from a neighboring monastery, and this meeting marked the beginning of a faithful friendship between the two.

As they walked along together, Romanus asked Benedict where he was going and what he planned to do. When he learned Benedict meant to be a hermit, he pledged to support him in any way he could. Romanus' community was above the gorge of the Anio River, on a cliff overlooking a hidden cave. He led Benedict to this cave, where the new hermit lived for three years. Romanus also gave him a *melota,* or sheepskin garment, and promised to keep Benedict's location a secret.

Ironically, Benedict's cave was near the former site of a luxurious pleasure villa and man-made lakes constructed by the infamous first-century AD Emperor Nero, whose persecution of Christians is vividly described by Tacitus in his last work, *Annals*. Modern scholars have questioned Tacitus' objectivity, especially because the ancient historian/senator had nothing but antipathy for Emperor Nero, but the passage below remains well known as one of the first non-Christian sources to mention Christianity.

In book fifteen, Tacitus maintains that after Rome's catastrophic fire of AD 64, and to squash rumors that the emperor himself had the fire started (so he could build a new city and name it "Neropolis"), Nero scapegoated Christians "to pacify heaven":

> Their deaths were made farcical. Dressed in wild animals' skins, they were torn to pieces by dogs, or crucified, or made into torches to be ignited after dark as substitutes for daylight. Nero provided his Gardens for the spectacle, and exhibited displays in the Circus, at which he mingled with the crowd—or stood in a chariot, dressed as a charioteer. Despite their guilt as Christians, and the ruthless punishment it deserved, the victims were pitied. For it was felt that they [the Christians] were being sacrificed to one man's brutality rather than to the national interest.[33]

This excerpt reveals a general Roman inclination to hold this latest sect of Judaism guilty of crimes against the state. Romans branded believers atheists who were rumored to participate in all sorts of sordid, even taboo activities, like cannibalism and incest (also orgies). Christians were colored in the public's mind with the same brush that branded the Jews as troublemakers for being anti-Roman-government activists.

The hedonism of Emperor Nero combined with his crimes against religious freedom left a deep mark on Christianity's history, and therefore, when Benedict situated himself near the ruins of Nero's resort and the aqueducts (begun by Emperor Caligula and finished by Emperor Claudius), Christ-like balance and agape love were being proclaimed in profound contrast to a long history of worldly self-indulgence and hatred associated with the location.

At great expense, Nero had dammed the Anio River here to make this resort, forty-four miles from Rome. *(Subiaco* is from the Latin *sublaqueum,* "below the lakes," a reference to these artificial lakes Nero had built.) Tacitus also damns Emperor Nero's reckless spending on artificial opulence:

> After the Rome conflagration, Nero profited from his country's devastation by building a new palace. Its beauty was not that of common, ordinary luxuries like gold and jewels. No, Nero commanded artificial lawns and lakes installed to make a pseudo-rusticity—landscaped woods here, open spaces and views there. These clever, impudent artificialities allowed Nero's architects and contractors to outdo Nature, and so they squandered an emperor's treasure.[34]

Among the shadows of imperial ego and waste, in a narrow, ten-feet-deep cave, Benedict started his deliberate, God-focused life. Here Benedict shunned the limelight that was the very air itself to one as egotistical as Nero. Another vivid early source on this emperor is *De vita Caesarum (Lives of the First Twelve Caesars)* by Emperor Hadrian's secretary, Suetonius, who shows the world the vanity of a weak Nero, describing him as blond, pretty- and pimple-faced, pale blue-eyed, squat-necked, big-bellied, spindly-legged, and reeking with body odor. Suetonius says Nero's health was amazingly good, especially considering the way he overindulged when he drank, and he adds that Nero's "greatest weaknesses were his thirst for popularity and his jealousy of men who caught the public eye."[35]

In Subiaco, Benedict became what he would later describe in the Prologue to his *Rule* as the second type of monk, the hermit, "trained to fight against the devil," building up "strength [in] the single combat of the desert." He became "self-reliant" and "ready with God's help to grapple single-handed with the vices of body and mind." Benedict could not have found a more poignant place in which to make a stand for God. And so this saint of land reclamation reclaimed his first area—a former imperial playground—for God.

CHAPTER 9

THE ROCK AND THE BELL

Romanus proved his friendship to Benedict during the hermit's years of solitude, first, by keeping Benedict's location a secret, and, second, by regularly bringing him a loaf of bread from his own slender rations. The precipitous, rocky drop between his monastery and Benedict's cave prevented Romanus from walking down to Benedict, so his routine was to remain on the stony promontory, kneel down, and tie a small bell and the loaf of bread onto a long rope that he slowly lowered down into Benedict's cave. The ding-ding of the bell alerted Benedict to the delivery of this gift of food.

As Gregory says, one day Satan—the old enemy of humanity—waited for Romanus, then hurled a rock at the bell as the monk let the bread down the cliff to his friend Benedict. This rock broke the bell, but Romanus was undeterred from serving God. He continued to take good care of the recluse, and for several years he was the only link between Benedict and the outside world. During this time, Benedict's animal-skin garb made him look like John the

Baptist. The once-privileged son of wealthy Romans was an unkempt hermit.

Benedict spent many unrecorded hours praying for others, fasting, and communing with God. He also used his time of solitude to fight the body's cravings. Gregory tells that Benedict was alone one day when the Tempter visited him disguised as a small blackbird that flew in his face. Benedict blessed himself with the sign of the cross, which sent the bird away. But afterward the hermit was painfully tempted by memories of a woman he had met years before in Rome.

The devil gave him a searing memory of her beauty. Young Benedict rehearsed in his mind her soft curves and carefree laugh, and was overcome by lust. Stirred by the idea of sex and pleasure, the holy man considered how wonderful it would be to leave the isolation of the wilderness and the rough cold floor of his cave for common earthly joys like a wife and the fulfillment of this intense body-hunger.

But—just as suddenly—God's grace brought Benedict to his senses. His mind cleared. Seeing a thick patch of briars and nettles beside him, he ripped off his animal skins, flinging his unprotected nakedness onto the sharp thorns of these dense bushes. He was thankful for their heavy, pricking needles, and rolled his longing in them, until his skin was lacerated. When he stood up again, his body was cut-covered, but this injured flesh healed his wounded spirit. Earth's thorns cleared the spiritual briars from his soul, preparing it for the seeds of goodness and abundant harvests of virtues. Benedict would tell his disciples he never felt tempted again. In its place, came an everlasting peace.

CHAPTER 10

SOLIPSISTIC HERMITHOOD?

I t was almost time for Benedict to emerge from his dark cave and illuminate the world, but he was not ready yet. He enjoyed his life as a hermit. He desired nothing but solitude and God, and was content with his life in the remote Subiaco cave. But he had begun to wonder if he was not becoming selfish. Thoughts began to tug him in the direction of the world: *Am I getting too much time alone with God? Is there such a thing as too much divine seclusion? Can permanent isolation start to dim the presence of God in me?* He started analyzing where humble hermithood ends and a proud solipsism begins.

Benedict had been living alone for so long that time had ceased to have its usual meaning. He no longer knew nor cared what day of the week it was, or which month. Easters came and went without his knowledge. He discovered his patient spirit did not require him to calibrate the praise of God in increments of anything but the eternal moment of Now. Benedict's contemporary Boëthius described this:

God abides forever in an eternal present, His knowledge, also transcending all movement of time, dwells in the simplicity of its own changeless present, and, embracing the whole infinite sweep of the past and of the future, contemplates all that falls within its simple cognition as if it were now taking place.[36]

Every day was Easter for Benedict, because he was always celebrating God's goodness. In the cell that was his Subiaco cave, Benedict came to understand in his every molecular cell, step, and breath that hours, days, and minutes do not belong to the human race. Time is not a possession we can pocket or in any way control. Instead, it is an illusion, even a trap, and an underlying theme of Benedict's *Rule* is that a peaceful earthly life is only possible when a person recognizes time belongs in God's hands. No one is the "King of Time". Surely this focus became real to Benedict as he sat on the hard dirt of his cave, not grasping at time but submitting to its limits and—in this submission—transcending earthly seconds.

His *Rule* teaches that the only true way to yield to time is by praising God and praying for others. This seems a far saner approach than the desperation most of us feel as we watch the wildly spinning clock hands, routinely calling out to each other, "There just aren't enough hours in a day!" or, "Where does the time go?" Daily we crave time to cram everything in—more seconds to talk on cell phones, exercise, read contracts, eat, give tests, fill in forms, go to meetings, catch buses, write e-mails, sign letters, run errands, type books, supervise homework, fly on jets, sleep, take vitamin pills, and get promoted.

Benedict's wise approach to time is one of the most attractive features of his *Rule*. Several times a day, every day of every week of every year, Benedictines stop whatever they are doing to acknowledge that their God is managing the world just fine without them for the moment, and, as they chant their gratitude, they realize their very thankfulness is more important to God than any other work they can offer. When they are finished, they go back to work, or go to eat, or lay down to sleep. They have bowed to God and to the time He holds in His hand, and in doing so, they make every moment eternal. This is the profound notion of time Benedict learned as he sat in his cave through the seasons of three years.

But it was almost time for Benedict to emerge from his narrow cave into the wide world, so, as Gregory tells it, one Easter Sunday around the turn of the sixth century, God appeared to a priest living not far from Subiaco and commanded him, saying, "You made yourself a delicious dinner, but did you know my servant Benedict is thin and hungry?" So the priest got up at once, packed his Easter bread, fruit, and wine together in a brown basket of woven vines, and set off with its heavy fragrance through a low valley above the rushing Anio River, in search of the holy man living in a crack of its steep hills.

After seeking for many miles, the obedient priest found Benedict in his cave, shouting out to him, "Come, brother. Eat with me. It's Easter!"

Benedict answered him, "Come in, come in. Yes, it's like Easter now you've come bringing the gift of your presence. Thank you for coming all this way. You brought a feast, too? What a double blessing!"

The priest corrected him, "No, Father, today is Easter, *literally*. The day we remember the Lord's Resurrection. God sent me to you in His goodness. Break your fast and dine with me. Let's celebrate together!" The priest began unpacking the meal.

"Is Lent really over?" Benedict asked, still a bit bemused. Then they said grace over the Easter feast. They ate with gusto and talked, and the conversation was as nourishing as the bread.

During this chat, the priest asked Benedict, "You've been isolated from the world long enough, haven't you? It needs you. Come back. Share what you know, Bennet. Help others." Then the priest returned to his church, taking dirty dishes with him in a much lighter basket, and Benedict was left to chew on the priest's visit and questions, his belly unusually full.

Not long after this, some shepherds happened on Benedict's cave. Spotting movement behind the bushes, they caught a glimpse of Benedict in his hairy animal-skin tunic and mistook him at first for a feral beast. But when they talked with the wild-looking recluse and came to know him better, they discovered his joyful, kind spirit and way of listening. As he described God's love for them, they abandoned their beastly desires for a life of love and eternal peace.

These shepherds could not but tell others about the spiritual blessings they had received from Benedict. Peasants and others started coming from all over to meet this hermit. The path to the entrance of his bare cave became more and more worn, and everyone who brought him earthly food took away spiritual nourishment. This was the humble beginning of the Benedictines, the tiny seed of genuine community from which many healthy monasteries would grow and mature over the next millennium and a half. Steadying this quiet movement through the turbulent intervening centuries of war-and-peace was the evergreen wisdom of Benedict's *Rule:* "For there is hope for a tree, if it is cut down, that it will sprout again, and that its shoots will not cease." Another reason for the movement's sinewy start was that Benedict's holy charisma drew in people from all walks of life—shepherds, peasants, pagans, monks, nobility, and eventually even royalty. From the very beginning, diversity was a signature trait of the Benedictines.

During these cave years spent meditating, eating herbs and whatever small fare Romanus dropped down to him, Benedict must have pondered the rough-and-ready John the Baptist, whom Jesus described to a crowd by asking these probing questions: "What then did you go out to see? Someone dressed in soft robes? Look, those who put on fine clothing and live in luxury are in royal palaces."

Benedict knew he had at least gotten that part of the spiritual equation right—like John the Baptist, he had chosen the path of poverty. But as he wrestled with his next step, he might have remembered other verses from Matthew's Gospel pointing to the public nature of John's ministry:

> In those days John the Baptist appeared in the wilderness of Judea, proclaiming, "Repent, for the kingdom of heaven has come near."
>
> This is the one of whom the prophet Isaiah spoke when he said, "The voice of one crying out in the wilderness: 'Prepare the way of the Lord, make his paths straight.'"[37]

This sixth-century Italian John the Baptist must have contemplated the amount of grounding in spiritual discipline that was required for someone who would teach others how to walk Love's way. Sitting alone in his cave, listening and worrying and praying to the God of infinite mercy, he might have said, *Lead me further along the path of blessing.*

CHAPTER 11

VICOVARO AND SUBIACO

Benedict's local celebrity grew. One day he received a visit at his cave from monks living in the monastery of Vicovaro, twenty miles down the Anio River. News of his power as a holy man had reached them, and, since their abbot had just died, they asked Benedict to replace him. At first Benedict refused. He believed they were insincere and would not live disciplined monastic lives.

Vicovaro's monks may have been lax in community for some of the same reasons as the later brothers—circa 1000—in the monastery of St. Clement of Pescara, on Italy's eastern coast. Medieval chronicler John Berard describes their absence of discipline in *Liber Instrumentorum seu Chronicorum Monasterii Casauriensis,* and it echoes Benedict's experience at Vicovaro: "The carelessness of some of the [former] abbots, and the lack of religion of the brothers, had brought the monastery to such great misery that hardly anyone could be found who wished to rule over them."[38]

However, the Vicovaro monks kept badgering Benedict, so he relented. But his grave misgivings remained. Coming out of solitude was hard enough for someone like Benedict who enjoyed his time alone with God. Adding to this difficult transitioning from the cave to community was that Benedict's worries as the new Vicovaro abbot materialized immediately. The monks there disliked his rules. Some were too proud to work, others were too obstinate to let their schedules be dictated by another, most were too sullen to submit to anyone but themselves, and many were simply too lazy to do anything but what struck them as interesting at that moment.

The ruins of this ancient monastery suggest its members might have prided themselves on the austerity of their living arrangements. Unlike above-ground monasteries, Vicovaro was a series of small caves carved into rock, each about eight feet (2.44 meters) high and six feet (1.83 meters) by four feet (1.22 meters) in size. Two larger caves served as chapel and refectory in this *laura,* a Greek word meaning "pathway" or "passage." From the fourth century on, the deserts of Egypt were filled with these underground, inter-connected monastic caves.

Perhaps the Vicovaro brothers believed living ascetically was work enough for them and that they should otherwise be left alone. They quickly grew angry with Benedict and his leadership. To and from the chapel and refectory, they paused in the shadowy stone corridors and whispered out a murderous plot, agreeing to hide poison in the young abbot's familiar cup of wine. When they presented it to Benedict before supper, he blessed the cup as usual, but it shattered as he made the sign of the cross, as if his blessing had been a sharp rock thrown against it. He realized the cup of wine was deadly, and that death could not stand up against the truth of the sign of life.

With a deliberate calmness probably more frightening to the monks under his care than any shouting could have been, Benedict reprimanded them, "May God have mercy on you and forgive you. Why did you try to poison me? Didn't I tell you this arrangement would never work out? Your lifestyle and mine don't agree. They never will. We must go our separate ways. I won't live here any longer."

Benedict left them. Shaking off the dust from his feet, he returned to his cave in Subiaco. He loved the wilderness and God's company, and was happy to live alone again.

But word spread quickly that the kind man of God was back, and people once again made their way to Benedict's simple cave. They were hungry for his words and frequent miracles. Soon he realized he must house these followers, so he left the cave at Subiaco for good, building first one monastery and then eleven others, all neighbors to each other. Each had twelve monks and a superior chosen by Benedict. He established a thirteenth one for those he believed would most benefit from living with and being mentored by him. He became the abbot of all thirteen.

Here in these first monasteries, Benedict began to work out the details of his *Rule*. The new father of monastic sons from widely different backgrounds probably studied the individuals in his communities and, in Gregorian fashion, saw they were the high-born and the peasant; the native and the foreigner; the educated and the illiterate; and they were young, middle-aged, and old, a community more diverse than today's average college dorm. In his cell, Benedict must have started writing down bits of his *Rule* as relationships played out, problems cropped up, and some approaches worked better than others. He also invested time during the *lectio divina,* reading and digesting other existing monastic rules, particularly the earlier *Rule of the Master.* He continued his organic note-taking for many years before finally finishing his *Rule* at Monte Cassino.

As Benedict's reputation for holiness continued to grow, Roman patricians began bringing him their children for education, so he established schools for them. Most notable among these first oblates were Maurus (twelve) and Placidus (seven), sons of the high-ranking Equitius and Senator Tertullus.

CHAPTER 12

MIRACLES OF LAKE AND SPRING

Gregory tells the story of Placidus, who walked down to the lake one bright day to collect some water for his brothers. But, because he was so young and easily distracted, he paid no attention to the lay of the land as he set his bucket down at a treacherous spot. Instead, he was watching a butterfly glide over the smooth, sparkling lake's edge when the shore crumbled beneath him, tumbling him headfirst into deep water, where the currents from a swift-running stream swept the child out, and—in one frightening instant—his bobbing head appeared as a speck from shore. Benedict was in his cell when he sensed Placidus was in gravest danger.

"Brother Maurus! Come! Hurry! Run as fast as you can. Go! Placidus went to fetch water and fell in the lake there. He's already far from shore. Quick!"

The teenager turned and bolted for the door. Wanting to please Father Benedict above all things, he ran down to the lake and kept running towards Placidus. Before he knew it, he grabbed the boy up by the hair and hurried back, his every muscle straining to save his friend. Maurus' feet snagged on a rock and he tumbled onto the hard shore before he realized, coming to himself and staring stupidly down at his wet sandals on the solid dirt, that he had been running on the water. This made him afraid, because he certainly had not meant to attempt something he could not in his wildest dreams do. He had only wanted to obey Father Benedict and be worthy of his blessing.

Maurus carried Placidus back to their spiritual father, still wondering with every squelch of his wet sandals, *How did I? Did I? What happened?* Placidus himself was too newly traumatized to talk and clung to Maurus on the journey home.

When Maurus told Benedict exactly what happened, Benedict said, "Ah, Maurus, your obedience ran you across that water, son."

"No, Father, it wasn't me. Your command gave me strength."

A friendly argument fed by their mutual humility stretched out between them, when young Placidus interrupted, "Hold on. I'll say what happened. Actually, it did happen to me. So listen. My nose was full of water and my mouth, and I felt tired and sleepy, my arms and legs were heavy, when all of a sudden out of nowhere I saw your hood, Father. I knew you'd come. So it was you all along! And thank you, big brother, for helping."

Benedict smiled down at Placidus. Then he tousled his hair, saying, "As the psalm says, out of the mouths of babes, Maurus."

Gregory also tells the story of the three monks who lived in several of the monasteries Benedict built on top of a soaring mountain in the Subiaco area, and how this precipitous location made the brothers weary going up and down, and down and up the steep slopes to fetch water from the lake below. Still, they had to have water, and, though they were good men, they were not above complaining. They got tired of clambering down the mountain's sharp sides, frequently slipping and falling and cutting their elbows and knees on loose rocks, then later hauling themselves back up, dirty and irritable, with heavy pails of lake water sloshing or spilling during the return climb. One day they visited Father Benedict, asking him to please move the monasteries elsewhere.

"Don't worry," he said. "Something good will happen."

They left grumbling, and that night Benedict took Placidus with him to climb that mountain. At the top, the Abbot stood and prayed. He prayed so long, in fact, that Placidus yawned, and then fell asleep sitting up, leaning against a boulder. Benedict picked three little rocks and placed them where he had prayed, to mark the spot. Then he woke Placidus, and they returned to the abbey.

The trio came again the next day, to complain of their Sisyphean task.

"Father, we must reiterate what a hard trek it is for us. Up and down that mountain. Up and down! It's dangerous, it's a waste of time. We've better things to do."

With a quiet strength in his voice, Benedict answered them, "Go on along now, back to the top of your mountain.

Look for three little rocks stacked on top of each other. Dig a little hole, that's all. And almighty God will start a spring there. I guarantee it. Go on. You won't have to fetch water from the lake anymore. Now, go on."

Without speaking, they left, grabbing a shovel from one of Benedict's sheds as they went, and they climbed their mountain once again, looking for the spot where the man of God had prayed earnestly for them and then had marked it with three rocks. Their mouths agape, they saw the very spot Father Benedict had directed them to—it was already sweating with moisture. With the shovel, they dug a small hole that immediately filled with the clearest spring water, and the water flowed and kept on flowing. They fell to their knees and scooped it up. They splashed it on their faces, and tasting it, whooped with joy, smacking their lips and clapping each other on the back. The youngest of them volunteered to run the shovel back to the father, and to thank him.

The water from that spring God made is gushing out of the top of that mountain to this very day, running down the length of its graceful sides toward the shining lake.

CHAPTER 13

A BORED MONK AND BAD BREAD

Often the abbots of Benedict's other monasteries asked him to help them with those in their care who were less-than-exemplary monks. One brother in particular could not sit still for times of prayer. He would rather be doing anything but praying. His mind wandered, he made to-do lists, he dreamed dreams, he worried, he remembered past pleasures. But he never prayed. In fact, he began leaving chapel when the praying started. So his abbot sent him to Benedict, who reminded him of the importance of prayer and returned him to his own monastery.

For a few days, the daydreaming monk did better, but he did not reform for long. Benedict's lecture was soon forgotten, and when the time for prayer came, he slipped out a side door of the chapel. His abbot sent a note to Benedict, to let him know.

Benedict promised him by return message, "I'm coming myself to check things out. Don't worry, brother. I'll sort it out."

And he did. Benedict visited and during chapel saw a dark, evil spirit in the form of a scowling young boy tugging the wayward monk by the hem of his habit out the door. Benedict was the only one who saw this, so he went back to his monastery and prayed for the monk again. The next week Benedict visited again. This time, he saw the lazy monk standing idle near the chapel as the monks filed in for Terce. Beside him was the same frowning companion, though the monk was again blind to his presence. The Abbot tapped the unsmiling boy on the backside with his staff. This so frightened Satan that he never again suggested to the monk that he should skip times of prayer and go for a wander. From then on, the once-disobedient monk loved singing the Psalter with his brothers. It became his favorite activity, and he would not miss it for the world.

For over two decades, Benedict led these monasteries in Subiaco, guiding the monks, teaching the children in the monastic schools, preaching in the monasteries and around the local area, serving the local community, and working miracles large and small. Those who knew him loved him. But trouble was on the horizon.

Not long after the Christian philosopher Boëthius was executed by the Ostrogothic King Theodoric around 525, followed the next year by the death of Theodoric himself, peace-loving Benedict found himself drawn into unavoidable conflict with his neighbor and fellow churchman, Florentius. After more than two decades of harmony and the pleasure of seeing his monasteries become well rooted in the Subiaco community. Benedict soon found that facing another's jealousy was one of the most difficult spiritual challenges he would ever handle.

The envious, coarse-tongued priest Florentius was furious that his neighbor, the soft-spoken Benedict, had a better reputation for holiness than he did. More followers congregated to Benedict than they did to him, and—since Florentius was not willing himself to make the effort to be holy—this mean-spirited man of God plotted to rid himself of a neighbor he considered a mere nuisance, an impediment to his own greater glory. First he tried to undermine the spiritual discipline at Benedict's monasteries by various devious means. He told lies about the Abbot to those living in Benedict's communities, but no one believed these, and in fact ignored them. So did Benedict. He knew they were untrue.

Then Florentius hit upon what he thought was a brilliant plan. He would put some poison in a loaf of bread blessed in church and given as a gift, a *eulogia,* a quite common, even universal sign of Christian fellowship. The priest rubbed his hands together, delighted as he contemplated his cunning scheme. Soon the limelight would be his alone to enjoy.

Benedict received the *eulogia* from Florentius with warm thanks, though he knew immediately the bread was toxic. Born with an "old soul," the Abbot had over the years honed this intense wisdom about humanity through his various interactions with people in Nursia, Rome, and Subiaco.

At suppertime that same day, Benedict's pet raven landed on his windowsill, waiting for his usual handfuls of corn from his friend. Benedict asked his feathered companion, "Will you take this? This loaf. Please. Go on, don't worry. Throw it in some bush where no one will find it and eat it."

But the loyal wild creature cawed, flapped his wings, paced along the ledge of the window, and otherwise did not budge. Ordinarily he was happy to come and go at Benedict's bidding, but he knew something was wrong with the bread and would not touch it.

Benedict understood his friend's natural hesitation and reassured him, "Yes, it's no good, now is it. But take it, go on, don't worry. Throw it somewhere isolated. For me, please?"

Finally, after more cawing and wing-flapping, and more reassurance, the raven obeyed. He took up the loaf of contaminated *eulogia* and flew off, searching three hours for a suitably remote spot. Finding it, he threw the bread down on the ground and returned. Benedict thanked him, "There you go, old friend. Your corn, and more besides. You've had a long journey. I thank you for ridding us of the poison of envy."

But Florentius would not give up easily. Realizing he could not kill the Abbot, he decided to put an end to the holy conversations among the monks in Benedict's monastery. The greedy priest hired seven shapely, long-silky-haired women to enter Benedict's monastery and cavort naked in the yard for all to see. And they did. They took off their clothes, joined hands, and danced with wild abandonment. Looking out his window, Benedict saw this and worried, especially for the younger brothers in his care.

He decided he must submit to the green rage of Florentius. Knowing there is a time to fight and a time to yield, he yielded. Benedict believed Florentius would stop terrorizing his monasteries if he himself left Subiaco.

But first Benedict had to put his houses in order. He appointed Maurus in his place, made sure every monastery had an able abbot who would obey Maurus, as well as a dependable prior, selected a few hardy disciples, and set off with them to an unknown destination. The footsteps of this monastic chartless voyager were nonetheless certain, as the sixth- or seventh-century monk-poet, Mark of Monte Cassino observed, because "Christ was your guide and your way."

Then something strange happened. When Florentius heard the news that he had indeed ousted the holy man named Benedict—his underhanded assault had succeeded—he rubbed his rough hands together and muttered a few indecent words expressing his pleasure. Then he did a little victory jig, jumping up and down on his balcony as he looked out over the horizon, envisioning the fame—all the ego-stroking—that would soon be his *with that bothersome abbot gone, and good riddance.* Throwing his head back, he growled with unholy laughter, when a loud creak sounded in the boards below him, and the heavy floor collapsed, crushing him completely in its fall. The rest of the house was left standing.

When Maurus heard this news, he was thrilled. He clapped his hands and jumped up and down, thinking, *If I can just catch Father Benedict before he gets too far down the road, they can turn around without delay. His enemy Florentius is gone. Our father can return. Life is good! The burden of leadership will be lifted from my inexperienced shoulders. We can return to normal. Florentius is gone! Forever!* He rushed down the Roman road, his sandals flying.

"Father Benedict! Florentius is dead! Dead! You can return!" Everyone began jumping up and down. All of the monks with Benedict cheered, happy to return to the Subiaco home they so loved.

But Benedict dropped to his knees, sad to hear his adversary had died, and in such a horrible manner. It also made him sad that one of his own monks would rejoice over the suffering of another. He gave Maurus penance to do, kissed him on the cheek, and blessed him, saying, "My path, Maurus, lies elsewhere. Yours is at Subiaco, my son."

The Abbot understood that he was meant to spread the Good News of God elsewhere in Italy. His journey continued. He also knew that changing places did not change his enemy. With a weary sigh, the forty-something monk contemplated starting over, hitched up the belt of his tunic and set out again, his eyes on the unwavering horizon.

CHAPTER 14

TURNING PAGAN RITES INTO MONTE CASSINO

After a few days of traveling on foot, Benedict and his weary band of monks found themselves seventy miles southeast of Subiaco. They had arrived in the once-thriving town of Cassinum, eighty miles south of Rome. But with the Roman Empire in shambles, so was Cassinum. To the west of them about a mile was the rocky hill of Monte Cassino, overlooking the Via Latina at an altitude of some 1,700 feet (520 meters).

Looking up, Benedict felt drawn to the mountains of this place. They pulled at his soul, and he told his monks they would build a new monastery there. This time, instead of thirteen individual monasteries, he would construct one larger one, to encourage even more cohesiveness and family spirit.

It did not take Benedict long to choose the right site. High above Cassinum, he discovered an ancient temple to Apollo. The people of Cassinum still worshiped this pagan god there, venerating Apollo as their god of healing, prophesy, poetry, dance, shepherds, and light.

Virgil puts a description of these religious rituals in the mouth of the *Aeneid*'s warrior Arruns, who prays, "Almighty god, Apollo, we your chief devotees heap up the blazing pine logs and walk through the middle of their flames to honor you, sure in our faith."

The first-century Roman poet Lucan has his own gruesome description of pagan woods:

> Not far away for ages past had stood
> An old unviolated sacred wood,
> Whose gloomy boughs, thick interwoven, made
> A chill and cheerless everlasting shade:
> There . . . barbarous priests some dreadful power
>   adore,
> And lustrate every tree with human gore.[39]

Benedict's first order of business was to smash Apollo's statue, overturn and destroy his altar, and burn the sacred grove where the ungodly sacrifices were made. Benedict then salvaged stones from Apollo's temple and recycled them to build the chapel of St. Martin on the same site. He also consecrated an oratory to St. John the Baptist where the pagan altar had been. (The remains of Benedict and his sister Scholastica are buried beneath the high altar of this oratory and are venerated here today.)

Less remote than Subiaco, the Mount Cassino monastery became an influential, much-visited ecclesiastical location. Benedict's preaching drew the citizens of Cassinum back to the place where they had sacrificed to Apollo, and they began to worship the God of this kind holy man.

Mark of Monte Cassino describes in verse how Benedict and his community transformed a wilderness of boulders and brambles into cultivated fields:

> Benedict, the mountain of Cassino does well to honor you,
> because you transformed it with your brothers, and made it something new.
> Its barren slopes are now like gardens shaped,
> its hardest rocks have turned into the ripest grapes;
> its cliffs can admire the crops that you will share
> with the poor, for the wildest woods now the best of harvests bears.[40]

But, as Gregory tells the story, Benedict's old enemy was outraged by the destruction of the pagan temple and appeared to the Abbot, screaming threats. The monks could hear the obscenities, but only Benedict could see the fiery mouth and glowing red eyes.

"Benedict! *Blessssssssss-ed* Benedict! I'll tear you apart. Rip you up. You'll wish you'd never been born. You hear me? Are you deaf as well as stupid?"

Benedict never answered him. This made the devil even angrier, and he chose more vicious words to hurl at the quiet abbot: "Maledict! Cursed *Maledict!* You're not *blessed!* No! You're damned! May you go to hell! Why do you torture me? Why persecute me? Burn my grove, will you? If you know what's good for you, you'll leave me alone!"

Benedict prayed a long time with this racket in the background. Then he sighed and made the sign of the cross, banishing the devil. The threats ceased at once. Although this battle was over, Benedict knew the war was not. More difficult spiritual combat would come, and he feared for his brothers especially.

Not long after the red-eyed devil cursed Benedict, the monks were constructing a new building for the monastery when they came to a huge stone they could not budge. Three strong monks put their shoulders against it, but it remained stubbornly in place on top of the mountain. More monks were called in, and they put their muscular shoulders against the boulder, but it still did not move.

The rock seemed rooted to the earth, as if it had grown to the very spot on which it rested. The monks realized the devil must be sitting on that stone, so they sent for the Abbot. The holy man of God came and prayed. Then he blessed the immovable rock and immediately two monks were able to pick it up and carry it off, as if it weighed nothing.

CHAPTER 15

WRITING DOWN A LITTLE *RULE*

E arly in his Mount Cassino abbacy, around 530, Benedict put his *Rule* to vellum. His decades-long contemplation of this work shows in every word of its brief prologue and seventy-three pithy chapters. Benedict probably continued to revise his *Rule* until his death. Written specifically for the brothers there, Benedict's *Rule* has wide appeal because it was originally intended for this diverse audience: the rich noble, the poor slave; the Roman, the barbarian Goth; the Christian, the pagan. It dialogues with them all, with anyone desiring intimacy with God, as the Abbot says in his prologue, "My words are meant for you specifically, *whoever and wherever you are*, wanting to turn from your own self-will and join Christ, the Lord of all."

Benedict's style also shows that he envisioned a universal audience for his *Rule*. He composed it—not in the erudite ancient classical Latin nor in the bookish scholarly Latin of his own day—but in the *Lingua Vulgaris,* the Latin spoken by the educated person of his time. His *Rule* sounds like the speech of an ordinary person, then, though its language is also graceful in every sense of that word. The young Roman student of rhetoric is always in evidence. He learned his lessons well, because, above all, the *Rule* is not preachy. Instead, its honest voice and kind simplicity draw the reader in completely.

This voice was honed during Benedict's Subiaco years. He never forgot the pure taste of God's goodness that he had experienced in his cave cell, and this genuine communion was inculcated into the *Rule* that guided his communities. Balance was the main aim—*ora et labora* ("pray *and* work"). In addition to the *Opus Dei,* Benedict stressed the dignity of work for all, both the wealthy and the indigent. In his day, this was a revolutionary idea. Those born into noble homes expected servants to manage the annoying minutiae of their lives, but in Benedict's monasteries, all tilled the fields, watered the crops, harvested the corn, weeded the gardens, worked in the kitchen, and served others in a variety of intellectual, educational, manual, or service-oriented ways.

His *Rule* also advocates divine peace. Living in a world of greedy Roman rulers, rapacious pagan Goths, and the concomitant bloodshed, Benedict would have viewed earthly combats as the outward sign of each person's invisible spiritual struggles between good and evil. His *Rule* teaches how to successfully fight these inner wars: "Give up your own will, once and for all, and pick up the strong, noble weapons of obedience to do battle for the true King, Christ the Lord." To this end, Benedict explained in concluding his Prologue, "We're going to found a school for the service of the Lord." For *school* here, he chose the Latin *scola,* a special fighting unit or *corps d'élite.* This military diction indicates that Benedict's monastery was not primarily a spiritual sanctuary or a place for intellectual growth, but a school training individuals how to bravely conduct and win the oldest war that each person wages: with "Me." Above all, the *Rule* teaches that prayer is the mightiest weapon and sincere kindness the strongest strategy.

With these objectives in mind, Benedict drafted his *Rule* by taking the most positive, humane approach to all the spiritual writings and monastic rules he had been reading over the years, hoping that he had "set down nothing harsh, nothing burdensome." He redacted past rules by St. Basil, St. Pachomius, St. Augustine, St. John Cassian, the *Rule of the Four Fathers,* the *Second Rule of the Fathers,* and the Italian *Rule of the Master,* mining them for spiritual gold and with a medieval humility, lifting extensive passages from the circa 500 *Rule of the Master,* with an eye to instilling compassion in his communities.

For example, the *Rule of the Master* frequently refers to God as a terrifying Lord, but Benedict emphasizes God as our Father, avoiding this anxious tone. The Master also describes eschatological concepts as God's punishment, but Benedict presents them in the positive light of God's mercy. He focuses on establishing equilibrium of soul and body to experience the "ineffable sweetness" of God's love. Some monks concentrated instead on asceticism, but Benedict did not want his brothers fasting 'round the clock, keeping red-eyed vigils the entire night, or working until they burned out. He wanted them to eat sensibly, pray and sleep regularly, engage in physical work about six hours a day, have set times for meditative reading, and even enjoy a summer siesta, if needed.

The early fifth-century *Lausiac History* by Palladius is replete with stories of desert ascetics. Once a hermit himself, its author had eyewitness accounts of monks who chastised their bodies. One ascetic, Macarius of Alexandria, ate nothing but raw vegetables for seven years and tried to conquer his need for sleep by not going near a bed for nearly three weeks. Macarius also punished himself once for a small fault by sitting out in the desert's Scete marsh, where the mosquitoes stung "like wasps," and "could even pierce the hides of wild boars," leaving his face unrecognizable from the swelling.

Years later, Palladius overheard the then one-hundred-year-old, toothless Macarius arguing with the devil. His austere practices had apparently failed:

> All alone, fighting both himself and the devil, he bickered: "What do you want, evil old man? Look, you've had oil and wine—what more can you want, you grey-haired glutton?" . . . "Do I still owe you any-thing? I've got nothing. Go away!" And, as though humming, Macarius kept repeating to himself: "You white-haired old pig, how long will I be with you?"[41]

Benedict sanctioned none of this austerity, and in its place he put community. The abbot was the father of the monastery, not its dictator. His *Rule* advises the father to lead *in collaboration with* the monks, by consulting them regularly. Chapter two describes the qualities of this leader:

An abbot who is worthy to be over a monastery should always remember what he is called, and live up to his name, because he is believed to hold the place of Christ in the monastery, as seen in his being called one of Christ's names, taken from the words of the Apostle: "You have received a Spirit of adoption [and] cry, 'Abba! Father!'" Therefore, the abbot should not teach or command anything that contradicts the Lord's teaching.

Benedict's *Rule* also respects children and the elderly, as well as the sick, paying special attention to their care, and it emphasizes that every guest must be treated as if he or she is Christ Himself. This wise instruction has lead to another signature trait of the Benedictines, their divine hospitality.

Gregory points out in his *Dialogues* that Benedict's own character is palpable when we read his *Rule:*

Although Benedict gained much recognition from his many miracles, the holy man was no less distinguished for the wisdom of his teaching. His *Rule* is remarkable for its wisdom and clarity of language. Anyone who wishes to know more about Benedict's life and character can discover in his *Rule* exactly what he was like as abbot, for his life could not have differed from his teaching.

Benedict's careful attention in his *Rule* to explaining the monastic virtues of obedience, silence, hospitality, chastity, diligence, and non-violent behavior does suggest the man himself. Its simplicity is his own. The fingerprints of his humility are in every line of this spiritual guide designed— not for mystics or superhumans—but for the average person wanting to commune with God and enjoy a more meaningful life.

Its opening call to obedience *("Obsculta")* suggests that "holy listening" comes first but is indivisible from action. The etymology of *obey* bears the weight of that principle, since the Latin *oboedire* can be analyzed into "Listen" (from *ob-*, "toward," and *–oedire* ((or *audire*)), "to hear"):

Listen, Child of God, to your teacher's wisdom. Pay attention to what your heart hears *(aurem cordis tui)*. Make sure you freely accept and live out the loving Father's directions. Working at obedience is the way to return to Christ when the carelessness of disobedience has taken you off-path. Follow Christ by wearing the strong, sacred shield of submission. Pray first before doing anything worthwhile. Then persist and never falter in prayer. God loves us as his own children, and forgives us, so we must not grieve him by rejecting that love and doing evil. We must always make the best use of the good things God gives us.

On every page we hear Benedict saying in this same caring, fatherly tone: "Pay attention. Surrender. Pray. Be kind. Stay humble." However, like most alert authors, Benedict felt his book was never really finished, and his *Rule*'s epilogue is a final call for humility. He reminds us that spiritual quests on earth, and even his own guidelines, are never "perfect": "Whoever you may be, rushing to your heavenly home, follow—with Christ's help—this little rule we've written for beginners. Only then, as God watches over you, will you ultimately reach the soaring heights of doctrine and integrity."

Translated into modern English, this "little rule" is under one hundred pages (and is less than 9,000 words), easily read before the end of an hour, but millions recognize its wisdom is inversely proportional to its brevity. This is the best lesson of Benedict's *Rule:* There is always more to learn. We are all always beginners. Kindness is never complete.

CHAPTER 16

HOW BENEDICT HEALS A BOY

The prologue of Benedict's *Rule* teaches that all human activities must be prefaced by sincere prayer, and the Abbot of Monte Cassino had many opportunities to practice this truth. One day his monks were busy laying brick to extend the height of a wall on the monastery's property, and Benedict was in his cell praying, when, as Gregory tells us, the old enemy appeared to the Abbot, insulting him, "Stupid man! You just keep on praying, while I go out to your equally stupid, crooked-wall monks and kill them all!"

Benedict sent a swift young man to warn his brothers, but as the message was being delivered, the dark spirit pushed against the new wall. It fell, and the thunder of bricks and still-wet cement crushed a young boy underneath their burden. He was the child of a curial, a Roman aristocrat, and well loved in the community. The older monks ran to him. Bending over his body, they cried, not knowing what else to do. No one noticed a long day of hard work had been ruined. They only cared that their young brother who had been alive a moment ago was now dead.

Their Abbot commanded them to bring the boy to him. At first they were not sure how to accomplish this, for the young body was entirely broken—his arms, his legs, all his bones, shattered. So they put him in a sack, as gently as possible, and carried him to Benedict. The Abbot told them to put the boy in his cell, on his cot. Then they lingered, their dirty faces streaked clean in places from tears. Benedict thrust them out and shut the door, to be alone with his grief, with the remains of the son who had called him "Father."

He prayed. *Never lose hope in God's mercy.* Shortly, the boy who had been crushed rose whole from the cot, tapping Benedict on the shoulder. The Abbot looked up with a tear-lined face, and the boy threw his arms around his neck, happy as ever to see his father.

"But, Father, why are you crying?"

"Never mind that now. Stand up with me."

Benedict pulled the boy up and looked at him, turning him one way and then the other to inspect his body front and back. Finding no scars, he began marveling. For a flickering moment, the holy man saw the earlier sieve in Enfide. It, too, had been completely broken, but it was also restored without blemish, as if it had never been damaged.

Benedict looked again at the smiling young boy and contemplated the power of prayer to heal and leave no scars. A verse from the apostle Paul's first letter to the Corinthians, quoted in his own *Rule,* came to mind, "[N]o eye has seen, nor ear heard, nor the human heart conceived, what God has prepared for those who love him,"[42] followed by another from Psalm 119, "It is good for me that I was humbled, so that I might learn your statutes."[43]

The older, wiser man and the young child stood together a moment without talking, and then Benedict calmly sent him back to the construction site, patting him lightly on his sound back, "Go now, son, help your brothers clean up the mess left by a wall that fell down."

"Fell *down,* Father?" His brown eyes grew large in astonishment.

"Yes, yes, there's been an accident today. Your brothers will tell you all about it. All is well. Go. Return to your work. Be brave, and rely on the Lord. God be with you, child."

"Yes, Father. Right away!"

He ran off.

CHAPTER 17

SCANT BREAD,
SCARCE OLIVE OIL

Benedict won spiritual battles, but wars continued unabated outside the walls of Monte Cassino, especially following Theodoric's destabilizing death in 526. Emperor Justinian and King Totila moved in to play tug of war with the ordinary Italian man, woman, and child, and death and famine rampaged.

As Romanus once gave from his slender rations of bread to an unknown hermit, Benedict and his monks shared their own supplies with anyone in the area who came begging. One day, however, Benedict found he had given away all the monastery's wheat and all but five loaves of its bread, for he had instructed the cellarer, "All guests who present themselves are to be welcomed as Christ," as also recommended by his *Rule,* which quotes Jesus, "I was a stranger and you welcomed me" (Matthew 25:35).

But when the Abbot saw his monks depressed to hear their supplies were so diminished, he gently reprimanded them for being cowardly. Then he comforted the brothers with these words, "Why are you worried about our lack of bread? Yes, today we have want, but, cheer up, tomorrow you'll have plenty to eat. Wait and see. Trust God."

Sure enough, the next day they found heavy sacks of meal before the door of Benedict's cell, some two hundred bushels, apparently sent by almighty God, for they never discovered what person had brought these to them. For this miracle, all the monks gave thanks. They learned from it that when they are in need, they should never doubt the abundance to come. Benedict's lesson that day in chapel was "God provides."

But one day the cellarer refused the last drops of olive oil to a visitor named Agapitus. A victim of the wars between Justinian and Totila, Agapitus was hungry, and his need made him unashamed to beg. But the cellarer turned him away, knowing full well he was breaking one of the Abbot's main rules. The monastery's cupboard had been depleted by the community's demands on it, with only a little oil remaining in a small cruet, but—with the illogicality born of scarcity—the cellarer would not part with it.

When Benedict heard Agapitus had been sent home empty-handed, he was angry. He went to the cellarer at once, demanding to see the olive oil. The cellarer produced several drops in a puny-looking vial. The Abbot asked one of his monks to throw the glass vial out the window. The cellarer gasped as it disappeared from sight, knowing it would shatter on the rocks outside. Benedict then told the cellarer to retrieve it. He was silent when he reentered the room, turning the cruet over and back in his hand, intact and unbroken, and with none of the oil trickled out. He never forgot this lesson: God's generous love is indestructible and complete, and we should follow His example.

The Abbot then commanded the cellarer to take the vial and give it immediately to Agapitus, reminding him, "Never be disloyal to God. Give to those in need. Don't be proud. Your way is not better than God's. Go on, son."

When the cellarer returned, Benedict asked his monks to pray. They thanked God for always giving the monastery what it required to thrive. The holy man was sitting near an unfilled, covered barrel, praying with his eyes shut. As he prayed, Gregory tells us that olive oil was gathering in the container, slowly rising with his earnest petitions. Then the golden liquid lifted up the cover and pushed it to the floor, and the escaping oil from the recently empty barrel overflowed, gushing onto and across the floor, and would not stop pouring.

When Benedict noticed, he quit praying and turned to the cellarer, "See what faith and humility do?"

The cellarer understood at once. He knelt before Benedict, confessing the weakness of his mistrust and disobedience and praising God's abundant mercy. Then, without being asked, he ran out of the monastery's gate, yelling, "Agapitus! Agaaaaa-pitus!" Finding him, he invited Agapitus back for buckets of oil, and the next day during one of the times of *lectio divina,* the cellarer meditated on these words of Jesus: "[G]ive, and it will be given to you. A good measure, pressed down, shaken together, running over, will be put into your lap; for the measure you give will be the measure you get back" (Luke 6:38).

CHAPTER 18

KING TOTILA'S FARCE

Benedict's fame as a holy man grew, but brought him no joy. Celebrity had never been his goal. Instead, he was increasingly distressed by the suffering caused by Emperor Justinian and the Ostrogothic King Totila. Soldiers came home crippled or not at all, and families everywhere were short of food, while these leaders were fixated on only one thing, how to raise money to win the war. Monte Cassino remained a haven in all this. Benedict made sure his monastery welcomed everyone—the hungry, sick, hurt, old, weak, mentally unwell, homeless, confused, or lonely—each person was invited in.

At the end of 542, the pagan King Totila was marching through Campania in preparation for an assault on Naples, when he heard of the holy man's miracles and power and felt a secret admiration for him. Benedict's influence rivaled his own, though in another sphere, for both were known as great leaders. Totila decided he would visit this Benedict, to see for himself. He ordered his servants to make arrangements.

"Let this simple abbot know the King of the Goths will call on him shortly."

All were Christ to Benedict, both high and low, king and peasant, and he sent a message back to Totila as he would to anyone, "You are most welcome. Come anytime."

But Totila decided to up the ante. To test the supposed prophetic powers of this Benedict, he would have one of his own bodyguards impersonate him. That would prove whether or not Benedict could tell the difference. So Totila sent for Riggo, one of his guards, and ordered him to put on the purple kingly robes and shoes. Then he gave "King Riggo" his horse and commanded the soldiers Vult, Ruderic, and Blidin to act as his retinue.

Somewhat nervous, the royal imposters and a legion of the king's best, most battle-hardened soldiers, gathered. The real King Totila slapped the muscular sheen of his horse's stately left flank to start them on their journey to Monte Cassino. He was proud of them. Their helmets shone in the sun, and their standards waved brightly. Their swords were sharp. They looked worthy of a great king. He smiled when he pictured the ruse they were going to pull. He was confident it would succeed.

As Riggo, Vult, Ruderic, and Blidin neared their destination, they saw the monastery high on a hill. They also spied an old monk sitting under a tree in front of it, reading a thick vellum manuscript bound in dark brown leather. Riggo cleared his throat a few times and pulled himself up straight on the too-large horse. The monastery was bigger than he had pictured it. His doubts deepened. But he had to obey his king's commands, so he dug his heels into the steed and rode resolutely on to meet the man in the plain tunic who had not yet looked up from his manuscript.

When the foursome was close enough for conversation with the old monk, King Riggo ordered Vult to alert this apparent doorkeeper, still lost in his reading, that royalty approached. But just as Vult opened his mouth to speak for his friend, Benedict looked up and smiled. Vult barked at the simply clad sixty-something monk, "Are you deaf? Can't you hear the grandeur of a king and his best legion? Is this the reception royalty receives? Where is the man called Benedict! Tell him King Totila is here to see him and won't wait!"

There was a long pause as the doorkeeper softly closed the manuscript, shutting his eyes also, as if he was memorizing some of its brown oak-ink words. When he opened his eyes, his voice was calm but firm. He did not look at Vult. He turned his steady gaze instead on the young soldier all in purple: "You are a faithful soldier, my good son, but you should take off those royal robes. They aren't yours, and I know it."

Riggo countered bravely, continuing in the kingly role, "What do you mean? Dare you insult a king? Who are you to talk to us like that?" He lifted the glittering regal sword from its outsized scabbard, then added, "Dare you not bow before us? Do you not know our power?" He gestured with the sword behind him, "Do you not see the strength of the men we command? Have you not seen the sharpness of their swords? Take a look and then speak properly."

Benedict continued quietly in the same even voice, "Did you really think you could fool me? I know your king is a mile away, waiting to hear from you how this trick played out. Come now, take those off."

Riggo's sword dropped to his side, smacking against the taut muscles of the king's black horse, which whinnied and pawed the ground fretfully as some of Totila's best soldiers pricked their own horses' strong sides sharply, fleeing in fear, and the once-determined faces of Vult, Ruderic, and Blidin were as pale as Riggo knew his own was. He realized in an instant this had to be Benedict himself, and dismounted quickly, flinging himself on the ground before the father. His cheeks burned red with shame. All the men remaining in that company of experienced soldiers leapt off their horses then and prostrated themselves before the Abbot, who said nothing as he went from soldier to soldier, helping them up and blessing each one with the sign of the cross.

They never recovered their tongues, but after Benedict had blessed them all, and his monks had brought them a snack of bread and wine, they mounted their steeds and rode off to tell King Totila how quickly they had been discovered.

CHAPTER 19

TOTILA'S GENUINE VISIT

As the successful, brave king listened to Riggo's tale, the jaunty smile faded from his face. He trembled. So Benedict was a true prophet after all, and he had provoked him. The humbled Totila asked his counselors what to do. He decided he must go to this holy man and apologize. He had met his match.

He rode alone to Benedict and dismounted at some distance from the monastery. Tying his tall steed to a tree, he advanced on foot to meet the monk, who was still sitting at the gates of Monte Cassino. King Totila recognized this simple, gray-haired man as the Benedict his soldiers had described to him, and he threw himself on the dusty ground without speaking.

Benedict got up and came to him. He stood over him, saying gently, "Get up, King Totila."

But the king could not move, because he was afraid. He was awed by this monk's presence.

Two more times Benedict urged the king to rise: "Come now. Get up, King. I do not require this. Rise and we will talk."

Seeing the king unable to stand, Benedict bent down to him and lifted him to his feet. Then he took Totila by the arm into the monastery for refreshments and conversation. Sitting across from the Abbot, the king finally recovered his voice, "Father Benedict, pray for me, a poor sinner."

Benedict took the war-roughened hands in his own, calloused by the hoe. He looked his new friend in the eyes, saying, "King Totila, you know my prayers for you do no good unless you yourself decide to change. You command thousands of strong men, but do you command your own self? You murder when you feel like it, and live sinfully. You give others much pain, and—what is worse—you enjoy it. You don't care if someone has no shoes. If another is hungry. If a soldier loses an arm in battle. Can you change? You must submit to a new King, to Christ, to the God of all creation, and to His Holy Spirit. You must be like a child. You must become a man of peace."

"Father, you yourself know I can't. I'm a man of war. My job is to defeat those who oppose my will. Do you know how many people count on me to win?"

"But you can be merciful, my son. You can spare those you capture. You can learn to love. You can become a kind ruler."

"If you say so, I'll try, Father. But bless me. I fear I can't change without your wonder-working prayers. You must promise you'll pray for me."

"I will. But you must surrender to a new Leader. This much you must do on your own."

"I will."

Benedict continued, "And know this. Some time from now, Rome will fall by the sword and be yours to govern." At this news, King Totila clapped before he had realized it.

Benedict held up one hand, "Wait." He continued, "But you have only nine more years to be a successful ruler-warrior. Ten years from now, you'll die overseas in battle. So plan the rest of your life wisely, and—as much as you can—be a godly king, Totila."

This second prophecy frightened the ruler. He begged Benedict to tell him better news: "Don't forecast my death, Father. Anything but that! I don't want to die! Don't say that!"

Then Benedict advised the king with a serenity Totila envied, "Anyone who believes in God and humbles himself before the Ruler of heaven and earth never has a reason to fear death. Become that man, Totila. With God's help, you can do it."

The king turned to leave, shaken by his conversation with the Abbot. But he remembered himself, and, turning back, he knelt before Benedict. "Father, now, before I go. Bless me. Please." This time, his hands were clasped humbly in front of him, his head bowed.

"In the name of the Father, and the Son, and the Holy Spirit, may you go out and live a changed life, King Totila. Serve the God of Peace. Love those you meet. Show mercy to those in your power. Go, my son, and be obedient to Christ."

Totila rose then on wobbly knees and walked slowly down the mountain path to his horse. When he returned to his camp, he was so deep in thought, no one dared approach him. He retreated to his tent and stayed there for hours, alone.

After his meeting with Benedict, King Totila did become known as a much more humane ruler, as the ancient historian Procopius noted, for example, in the pagan king's offer of generous terms to those conquered at Naples in the spring of 543. Benedict's prophecies for him also came true. Several years after Totila's interview with the Abbot, he captured Rome in 549. Then, in the summer of 552, the Goth king died in the battle of Taginae, ending the fierce wars between the Ostrogothic Kingdom in Italy and Roman Byzantium.

CHAPTER 20

GREED AND A LAMP

Aside from the occasional royal visit, the bulk of Benedict's life was taken up with the quotidian, the way most people's lives are. Sometimes monks did not like sharing, or they found the servant's role a difficult one to accept. He also met the occasional hard-hearted nun.

Benedict dealt with all acts of disobedience personally, because he felt responsible for the souls in his care. To this holy man of God, the boundary between himself and another was not a solid wall, but the inclusiveness of Christ; therefore, another's problem was his own, for Benedict believed the salvation of his soul depended on loving others and helping them. The abbot's role was carefully outlined in his *Rule:* "He must be chaste, peaceable, and merciful. He should always embrace mercy over judgment (James 2:13) so that he may himself win mercy." If an abbot had to punish a brother, Benedict advised in his *Rule* that he should "avoid extremes," because these might harm a soul, just as a too strenuous rubbing to remove rust from a bowl can break the bowl instead.

Gregory's story of the servant Exhilaratus and his delivery of wine demonstrates the character an abbot must have. One day Exhilaratus (who would later become a monk) was sent by his master to Benedict with two wooden flasks filled with wine as a gift for the Abbot. As he started out, Exhilaratus was already licking his lips and considering what a tasty present the two containers would make for the Abbot.

By the time he neared Monte Cassino, Exhilaratus had convinced himself that he had to be allowed to keep one of the wooden flasks for himself, because, he reasoned, *I'm hot. I've walked such a long way in the heat. And whoever notices me? Who applauds my work? Besides, my master's gift is simply too much wine for one person. Who does this Abbot Benedict think he is? What a glutton!*

Greed muddled his thoughts, until Exhilaratus decided he would be doing his master and Benedict a favor if he kept one flask for himself. *I deserve it. No one ever gives me what I need. Sometimes you just have to take care of yourself, and rules go hang,* he thought, squatting to stash one of the flasks in a bush. Standing up, he hoisted the remaining flask in his arms, plastered a smile on his face, and readied a greeting for the Abbot.

Bowing low, he presented the gift to Benedict, who was not fooled. He could see the cloudy behavior advertised in the man's downcast, side-glancing eyes, and too-eager words: "Great Father Benedict, your most excellent reputation precedes you everywhere, and—here—please accept this best of all wines, given by my superior to you, the best of all abbots."

Benedict took it, saying simply, "Thank you. My brothers and I will enjoy this kindness." But as Exhilaratus turned to leave, Benedict warned him, "Be very careful, my son, not to drink that wine you hid in the leaves of the bush outside this monastery's gates. Instead, open it up, and pour it on the dirt. You will see what your avarice has gained you."

These words stunned Exhilaratus. Holding his tunic, he ran from Benedict's presence, embarrassed and unable to defend himself with words. But because he was curious to know whether the Abbot was telling the truth, he retrieved the stolen flask of wine from the bush. It looked just the same to him. Glancing over his shoulder to see if he had been followed, Exhilaratus remembered his earlier plans to enjoy the flask's contents all by himself, but something in the Abbot's compelling words made him open the wine and, with a sigh, start emptying its ruby contents.

As it splashed on the ground and pooled at his feet, Exhilaratus was again overcome with a longing for that sparkling liquid. The saliva gathered in his mouth. Angry with himself for listening to that silly abbot, he convinced himself that only he himself knew what was best for his soul. He stopped pouring and hugged the flask to his chest: *It's impossible to share everything in this world, now isn't it. Impossible!* Curling his full lips into a sneer, he continued: *"My brothers and I will enjoy this." Well, good for you, holy man. But as for me, myself, and I, we'll enjoy this wine all alone!*

Exhilaratus smiled. His eyes glittered with the promise of getting. As he brought the remaining wine to his moist, pursed lips, a venomous snake slithered out of the flask and dropped on the ground into the muddy puddle, splattering his tunic blood-red. The servant immediately recognized his mistake—Abbot Benedict had been right. For the first time in this servant's life, he was frightened by his own lusts. He had tasted the bitterness of greed, and now knew it was nothing but a toxic thirst. He threw the flask down and ran from the snake and its poison, realizing he should learn to hunger instead for self-control.

Benedict also had to deal with a monk who was having a hard time with the monastery's required servanthood. Brother Jude came from a noble home; his father was a famous Roman politician, and Jude had grown up on an estate run by slaves. Benedict discerned that his aristocratic background was constantly rebelling against the humble tasks assigned to all the monks. He also remembered that Jude had entered Monte Cassino filled with an idealistic fervor that quickly dissipated when it ran up against the ordinary tilling of the soil, the daily weeding of the garden, and the mundane service in the kitchen. Benedict saw, too, that Jude had the gift of a keen, orderly mind but that his spiritual progress was impeded by the ignorance of pride.

So one day Abbot Benedict asked Brother Jude to hold the lamp for him at suppertime, a task rotated among the monks. Most enjoyed this simple work because it gave them a chance to be near the Abbot. To be beside Father Benedict and overhear his conversation was an education and a blessing for the soul, and those who hungered to be close to the father's kindness were honored to do anything, no matter how small, if it allowed them to be near him.

But Brother Jude found this menial task irritating. As he stood behind the Abbot and held the lamp to light the father's simple, meatless meal, Jude reflected on his former life in his own father's house, where servants stood behind him and held the lamp for him. The memory rankled. He remembered hands that dressed him, plowed the fields for him, and did the kitchen chores for his family, and a scowl pulled his thick black eyebrows down into the bridge of his aquiline nose.

Jude bit his full lips, complaining to himself, *What am I doing here? All know my father in Rome. This is ridiculous! Who is this old man, this lowly monk! How can he expect me to hold the lamp for him? He should get someone else to do this stupid job. I should be doing more important things than holding candles!*

Because Benedict was wise, he overheard these proud thoughts. He turned to Brother Jude and challenged him, "Do you *still* think that way? Make the sign of the cross over your heart, my son. Ask God for forgiveness. The devil is tempting you to harden your heart. But don't be insecure. Don't let arrogance rule you. It has no place here. Let the Savior ride His donkey through your heart, and you will see Him on the Cross."

Benedict then dismissed Brother Jude and asked another monk to hold the lamp for him. As Jude turned to leave, the father gave him this command, "Go to your cell, son, and think on the things I've told you. Pray to understand the importance of lamp-holding in Christ's kingdom. No task is small when Love performs it."

Brother Jude left the Abbot's table, shoving his way through the seated monks who were eating with the quiet attentiveness of those who knew something embarrassing had happened. Jude pushed past them, his face flushed. A couple of his friends whispered as he passed by, breaking their Benedictine silence—"What's up?"

Jude spat out, "Stupid lamp!—Ridiculous!—I have every right—!"

They understood immediately and realized the sagacious father was able to read their unspoken thoughts. Each one of them chewing fresh bread at the suddenly deeply silent tables found it turned dry as dust in his mouth, and tasteless. One by one they stopped chewing. Each felt silently admonished for his own unique, hidden complaint, nurtured by the same spiritual smugness. Brother Jude was not alone, and Benedict knew this, too.

CHAPTER 21

IMPOLITE PRIDE

Pride is always found in rudeness. Benedict saw this truth lived out, sadly, by two conceited nuns who mistreated their faithful servant. These nuns were Benedict's neighbors. They lived at home, and both were from the best families. Their noble background had, however, bred ignoble minds in them. In other words, they saw themselves superior to others and therefore believed that they were allowed to say whatever they wanted, whenever they wanted, in whatever manner they wanted. They had not learned that humility and politeness are God's best friends.

These nuns had hired a man to run their errands for them. He had been a servant in their family ever since he was a child. For that reason alone, they should have felt some warmth toward him, but they did not. To them, he was a thing that goes and brings. They regarded him with no more curiosity than they would have a hammer. Both he and it were merely tools. This manservant also loved God and wanted to serve the Lord by serving these nuns well; however, he was finding their put-downs made him angrier every day.

He heard that Father Benedict understood such matters, so he took his problem to the Abbot, saying, "Father, I'm at the end of my rope. Those sisters cut me to the quick. Treat me like scum. I've been patient, years. They always find fault. If I bring a message from another sister, I don't bring it fast enough. If I bring supper, it's not hot enough. Other times, it burns their tongues. No vegetable's fresh. All fruits are sour or soft. Nothing's right. I know I'm not perfect, but I work hard. And they never thank me. They don't even know my name. They call me 'Boy,' and, Father, you can see I'm no longer what you would call young."

Benedict visited the nuns. He reprimanded them for their arrogant behavior: "Don't you know I myself came from a wealthy home like you? That's no reason to feel superior. God doesn't view the world like that. Remember? The first are last, the last first. Change your ways before it's too late. Your servant's name is Peter, by the way. Be kind to him. You must talk to him as if he is Christ Himself. Get control over your tongues, Sisters, for where the tongue goes, the heart follows. If you curse others, your life is cursed. If you bless others, your life is blessed. Remember this. If you don't change, I'll have to consider you both excommunicated."

But the sisters did not change their behavior, and both died not long after their conversation with Benedict. Yet God is always merciful, and so was his representative, the Abbot. When Benedict heard the two nuns had died excommunicate, his heart softened on their behalf. He sent word that he had offered an oblation for them. They were forgiven. For the kindness of God is mysterious and deep, and his love is everlasting.

Although the greater part of Benedict's work was involved in ordinary pastoral responsibilities, it was not restricted to the commonplace. Sometimes he was called, Gregory tells us, to unique tasks like exorcism. One day, Constantine, the Bishop of Aquinum, sent a possessed clergyman to Benedict. Constantine had tried everything he knew to help this young man—had sent him on many pilgrimages—but nothing worked. He appealed to the Abbot, "Can you help my friend Simon? You're his last hope. I'll send him to you under heavy guard. Father Benedict, you should have heard him preach when he was sane—what a beautiful voice he had, every intonation full of meaning, every tone sonorous. He was once a rising star in the Church, till he lost his mind."

As soon as Benedict saw the man, chained at the wrists and ankles, he recognized that in this clergyman the demon pride had been allowed to run to extraordinary lengths. The man had spent his life in love with his own voice and concerned with ecclesiastical status, surely the greatest irony of them all, Benedict reflected, and this obsession had driven his soul to insanity. He was scratching himself like a dog. His body was covered in self-inflicted wounds, and the heavy chains were powerless to stop this. They merely kept him from running away into the woods.

"*Iesu Christo Domino, preces fundens,*" Benedict began. Then louder, "Brother Simon, I can help you through God's power, but you must listen to me."

"We are listening," growled the clergyman, spitting on the Abbot's tunic.

"You must give up your desire to be highly placed within the Church of God. You must stop eating meat and indulging in the pleasures of the flesh. You must live a life of humility among the brothers. Stop lusting after holy orders. Don't take the sacrament of priesthood. If you dare reenter the hierarchy of the Church, you'll be doomed by your pride. May the Lord heal you and free your spirit. Blessings on you and on your suffering, my Son."

The Abbot's words penetrated Simon's lunacy. He became clear-headed for the first time in years. He heard and obeyed the Father's wisdom. Gone were the pain of madness and the voices constantly snarling. He obeyed for days, then months. His head stopped hurting. The sores on his body healed completely. He was no longer frightened. He welcomed this peace. It allowed his body to rest.

But the years passed, and Simon's spirituality never advanced beyond the surface of his soul. He did not learn to submit to God daily and began, little by little, to notice that many men younger than he were starting to advance through the ranks of the Church. While he wore his simple tunic, they quickly surpassed any ranking he ever held. He became jealous of their accomplishments and positions and felt diminished. The humble service he was assigned seemed utterly ridiculous. Whenever news came to his ears of another's success, his cheeks burned with envy, and even the simplest chore, like milking the cow, became impossible.

Simon stared at his shaking hands, then at the wooden bucket half-filled with creamy milk. Jerking himself up, he knocked over the bucket with one strong kick, spilling its healthy whiteness onto the spongy brown ground. His hands twitched as he watched it melt into the earth. Pacing up and down beside the upturned, dripping bucket and the cud-chewing cow, he fumed aloud:

Bishop! Barbato made Bishop! He never could hold a candle to my preaching. And look at me. A middle-aged man with no future. Going nowhere. My audience, this beast. I must be ordained. He can't stop me. People will flock to hear me speak. I'll show Barbato a thing or two! I'll climb! I'll succeed! I've always been destined for greatness!

Sadly, Simon turned his back on Benedict's godly advice. That very day he left the cow half-milked, stripped off his humble tunic, and stalked off in search of fulfillment for his outsized ego. Pride possessed him the rest of his life. He never found the audience he craved, and died like a beast, covered in open wounds, scratching himself, howling indecipherable things into the lonesome night.

CHAPTER 22

TARRACINA

While Benedict was abbot of Monte Cassino, many visitors—rich and poor—traveled along the Latin Way to seek him out. They came to hear him talk of God. One of these visitors was an elderly, affluent Roman who approached Benedict after one of his sermons. He offered to give him his estate near Tarracina, a seaport some thirty miles west of Monte Cassino. The Abbot thanked him, saying he would prayerfully consider this generous gift and give him an answer soon.

"Please, Father, say 'Yes.' Why delay? Accept my land. It would ease the burden of my soul to help in God's work after a life squandered chasing after mammon. I'm sick of it. I want to make peace in my soul."

Benedict assured him he would spend time in prayer contemplating this possibility. The nobleman was struck by the curious rhythm of the Abbot's life and by the independence of his soul. For who would not grab a gift of real estate? *Apparently, this monk,* he told himself as he rode home. As Benedict spent several days in prayer over the matter, the rich nobleman spent these same days contemplating Benedict, a man who would not be bought, who did not strive to ingratiate himself to the world. Both qualities made a lasting impression on the businessman.

After many days, Benedict felt a peace in his decision, and sent a message to the nobleman that it was indeed God's will for a monastery to be built on his estate near Tarracina. Benedict then picked a dozen seasoned monks to start the new monastery on the coast. He also selected an abbot and a prior. Although the brothers did not complain, Benedict knew they were unhappy to be chosen for this mission. They loved Father Benedict and did not want to leave him and their comfortable lives at Monte Cassino. He reassured them, "I know your hearts are heavy with leaving sorrow. Mine is, too. I hate to see you go. But, don't worry. God is with you, and I'll come to you soon. Go on, confident in Christ. I'll come in a fortnight and show you where to build— where your cells should be constructed and the refectory and the oratory. We'll walk through it all together. You'll not be alone in this."

The days went by quickly, for there was much to do. The Tarracina monks scouted out the land and also got acquainted with the people of their new coastal community. On the thirteenth day after their departure from Monte Cassino, the day before the Abbot's announced visit, the monks prepared food and straightened up their tents in anticipation of Abbot Benedict's arrival the next day. Their camp buzzed with excitement. Meanwhile, back in Monte Cassino, the monks wondered how Benedict would fulfill his promise of traveling to help the Tarracina monks, for he was exceptionally busy with duties there, at home.

That evening, the Tarracina abbot and prior had a strange dream. In this dream, Benedict came and showed each of them where to construct the different buildings for the new monastery. In fact, Benedict walked each brother around the very grounds of Tarracina and pointed out this spacious knoll for the oratory and that level area for the refectory, and, near both, a perfect spot for the living quarters.

But when they woke up, both discounted this vision, and dismissed it. Then they remembered that Father Benedict was coming that day and would show them where to build. But they waited all day, and the Abbot never came. Disappointment clouded the heart of each brother. The abbot and the prior were especially lost. Feeling betrayed, they set off for Monte Cassino, for an audience with Benedict.

"Father, you said you would come, but you didn't!" complained the Tarracina abbot.

"We *don't* know what to do! The task is too huge, Father!" echoed the Tarracina prior.

"But I did come to you, my sons. I did. Remember the night before the fourteenth day after your leave-taking? You were expecting me the next day, remember? Have you forgotten how I came to each of you that very night and showed you where to build?"

They looked at each other simultaneously, eyes wide, before exclaiming with one voice, "Father, forgive us for doubting you!"

"I see now," said the abbot of Tarracina.

"So do I," affirmed the prior.

"We must go," they told Benedict. "We have much to do."

They returned and built exactly as Abbot Benedict had instructed them to do in their dreams. All the monks, both at Monte Cassino and Tarracina, marveled at this miraculous communication.

CHAPTER 23

THE POOR AND OPPRESSED

One of the reasons Benedict was so busy in Monte Cassino was that he spent a great deal of his time paying attention to and meeting the needs of the poor. Broken by war and ravaged by famine, those born with little grew up to inherit even less; meanwhile, the Abbot watched the rich grow richer and blinder to others' needs. This unfairness made Benedict work to alleviate the pain of those who came to him destitute.

Benedict also knew that sometimes good people get caught by misfortune and pinched into financial hardship, no matter how diligently they work. He understood that the greed of those born into affluence often contributes to the suffering of those below them. One day, a gaunt man with thickly calloused hands came to Benedict. He had heard the abbot was kind, and identified with the problems of ordinary men and women.

"Father Benedict, I humble myself before you. It's not easy for me to be here, but, as you can see, I'm a poor farmer. I've had, my family and I, only a few small meals these past few months. The earth is unforgiving, hard, the rains don't come, but wars and taxes always do. My nest egg is gone, my family, Father, is hungry, and I owe my creditors twelve pieces of gold. Twelve! A year's wages! Might as well be millions! They're threatening to throw me in jail. If I lose my job and all hope of working again, what chance does my family have of eating?"

Benedict furrowed his brow in concern. "My son, I'm sorry to hear of your distress, and your family's. I want to help you; but times are difficult everywhere. At present, I don't have even one piece of gold to give you. But come back in two days. Take a sack of grain to keep you till then. And I'll pray. Something will turn up. It always does. Try not to worry. No one will harm you. You were wise to swallow your pride and come here."

As commanded by Benedict, the faithful, poor man returned to Monte Cassino on the third day. The Abbot was beaming, "My son, look!" Though weary, the farmer ran to the Abbot, who was holding out—not twelve—but thirteen pieces of gold.

"What? How? For me? All this . . . for my family?"

"Yes—here, take it—as I was praying this morning, I thought I'd go check the corn chest. We're always giving out corn from that chest, and more always pours in. I wanted to see how much was in it today to give you and your family while you get back on your feet. I was hoping we had a generous amount to keep you a good long while, so I took some brothers with me to scoop whatever was there into sacks for you. As I was walking that way, pondering the greater problem of how to pay off your crushing debts, I saw something shine out from the corner of the barn. At first I thought it was a chink of sun coming through a hole in one of the wooden planks. But, as I got closer, I saw, and the monks with me saw, thirteen gold coins, and we knew they had been put there for you. Do take them. Use twelve to pay off your looming debts, and have something substantial leftover to buy whatever else your family needs. Get up. You've thanked me enough. Thank God once you get home with your family. Go now. Be full of joy. Get up. Go with God's blessings."

And that hungry farmer with the recently shriveled-up hope found his skinny legs dancing out of the gates of Monte Cassino. Skipping down the road to home, thirteen bright coins jingling in his sack, dust flying behind him, he sang, "Clap your hands, all you peoples; shout to God with loud songs of joy" (Psalm 47:1).

Sometimes, however, criminals showed up at the gates to Monte Cassino, where they were met by Benedict's gate-keeper. He was old and wise, as those who open spiritual doors for others ought to be. As Gregory tells the story, this gatekeeper was especially discerning because years before, the Abbot had delivered him from the devil. The devil had ridden past disguised as a veterinarian *(mulomedicus)*, entering this godly man on a whim as he was drawing water. Caught off-guard, the then middle-aged monk was cast to the ground, thrashed this way and that, until Benedict came along and firmly slapped him on his shoulder with his hand, forcing the devil out and bringing his good friend back to his senses. The name of this now silver-haired gatekeeper was Marcus, and he had a long memory for gratitude.

Therefore, when Marcus heard a commotion outside the gates of the monastery one hot summer day, he opened the doors immediately to see who was in need. Shouting out, as he always did, "Thanks be to God!" he encountered the most astonishing sight. Rearing up on a proud stallion countless hands high was the infamous Goth, Zalla, one of Totila's captains, an Arian heretic well known for persecuting priests and monks. But Marcus neither flinched nor budged. Not taking his eyes off this thug, he motioned discreetly for his assistant to fetch the Abbot.

The gatekeeper knew that Zalla especially hated believers, but was also known for deriving pleasure from making anyone suffer. He would torture to death those who so much as looked at him wrong. Peasants who had the ill-fortune of meeting him on the road to Tarracina always stared at the dirt clods under their feet until the loud clomp of his heavy-hooved, well-fed horse was well past, while priests and monks found any chance meeting with the pagan fatal.

Marcus saw Zalla's current victim was a farmer named David, a peasant whom—he guessed—the brute had rounded up on the pretext that the man owed him money. Extortion was this barbarian's favorite pastime. And Marcus was right. An hour earlier, Zalla had tied David's hands behind his back, held a hot torch to the poor man's head, and rummaged through his clothes for a bulging purse or a full pocket. The man's courage had cracked when he smelled his scorching hair, and he had fabricated a confession, "I've got no money here, Captain Zalla, only a shovel, kitchen tools. I gave my money to that holy man, Father Benedict. If you want it, go see him. He has it all."

This desperate plea was meant to gain the peasant a few minutes' reprieve from the horror of Zalla, and it worked, though the soldier had answered him by throwing down the torch to light David's hut on fire. Then Zalla used strong ropes and clever knots to tie his captive's trembling hands behind his back and to the impatient, prancing steed. The farmer looked like a small rabbit lashed to a raging lion. Mounting his horse in one strong motion, Zalla shouted down to his shocked hostage, "Okay, lead the way. Take me to this Benedict. I'll grab the gold of his holiness—ha!—and then I'll kill him, too!" Zalla whipped the back of the bent priest with the loose end of the rope, starting him forward. The fiery breath of the barbarian's fierce stallion seared the neck of the stricken prisoner, who began what he considered his death march towards Monte Cassino.

An agonizing stretch of time later, David counted himself fortunate to reach the gates of the monastery, his neck bleeding from horse bites. Zalla struck his captive one more time for good measure and shoved him to his knees with a kick to the middle of his spine. Only then did he look up. He saw a spindly old man with his arms crossed, staring him in the eyes, and, behind him, another white-haired monk, his eyes closed as if sleeping. Zalla guessed that the one standing there with head bowed and eyes shut was the

Abbot he had heard so much of. So he screamed at that one, "Hey, old man! Wake up! You hear me? Give me this man's money. I've come for it! Or I'll kill him! Then *both* of you!"

Gray-haired, but still straight of back, the man of God stepped out from behind Marcus without looking at Zalla. Instead, he stared at the thick ropes binding the farmer. They immediately dropped to the ground. The captive was free but did not know it yet. His body bent, his hands behind his back, he kneeled still, forehead and nose in the dirt.

It was Zalla's turn to be shocked. For once, he was nonplussed. His cruel mouth twisted and agape, he gawked at the messy pile of ropes. He was a man who specialized in torture. He knew the cords lashing the priest to his steed had been loosened far faster than any hand could untie them. Zalla fell off his horse then, and, with the humility of a Totila, prostrated himself before the man he had heard called Benedict, convinced he was in the presence of a power greater than his own.

"Pray for me, good sir. Pray for me!" he shouted in the dust, coating his lips with it, tasting the earth.

The holy man turned to Marcus, and nodded toward the peasant. Then he turned to David, "Come, my son. Stand. Let Marcus help you. He's far stronger than he looks, I promise. Your brothers will clean your wounds and give you food, then you can sleep all you want." Marcus put his arm around the injured man and escorted him inside.

Benedict then faced Zalla, who begged him, "Please, don't—don't kill me now! Have mercy on me, Father!"

"Get up, Zalla. My monks will give you something to eat. Then we'll talk about the serious matter of your penance. You must mend your murdering ways. You must stop bullying. Your way of life brings others only pain, and yourself." Zalla was invited to the Abbot's table, where they spoke of spiritual sustenance, and, like Paul the apostle, Zalla was converted and followed God along a new path of kindness.

CHAPTER 24

RESURRECTION CHILD

One day Benedict was in the field working with the brothers to harvest the corn when a simple country man approached the monastery gates, carrying a little limp body in his arms. Tears coursed down his cheeks and fell drop by drop in the dirt, like rain. He cried out over and over, "Father Benedict! Give me back my son! Father Benedict! Give me my son! Oh, my son!"

Marcus recognized the sound of grief and threw open the monastery's gates. "Blessings, brother," he told the man, "the Abbot is in the field harvesting the corn. He's not here," pointing off to the right.

Gently, the father laid down the body of his dead child by the gates of the abbey then and ran in the direction of the cornfield. The red dust rose under his sandals. He felt he could not go fast enough. Benedict was already making his way back from a day of hot work under the merciless, unstinting sun.

They met halfway. The grief-stricken father shouted at Benedict from a distance, "Give me back my son!" He slumped to the ground and on his knees pounded the silent air with his fists, screaming his prayer, "Give me my son!"

The man of God was stunned by this request. He walked on silently until he was standing in front of the wet-faced father. Benedict asked him then, "What do you mean? Have I taken your son from you?"

"No," groaned the father. "He's dead. Don't you know? You must bring the one I love back to me!"

Benedict was overcome with compassion, but lamented, "Why ask me something so hard? Why put such a heavy burden on me? I'm just a man! I'm no apostle! My weakness can't bear this! It can't! I can't do it!"

The father hugged Father Benedict around the knees, clinging to him. His cries were muffled in the coarse cloth of the father's habit, "I won't leave here till you do."

Benedict stood completely still as the tears soaked like blood through the rough cloth, burning his legs. Putting his hands on the father's shaking shoulders, he knelt down in front of him, and hugged him to himself. Sighing, he gave in to the father's anguish and to the hopelessness of the situation, saying, "Okay. Where is he then?" They stood.

"At the gate, Father."

Benedict and his brothers went to the gate then. The Abbot was thinking, *God will provide. But how?* The father asked them all to pray with him as he knelt down beside the lifeless child, his hand on the small chest. Then Benedict stood up, stretching his hands toward heaven, imploring, "Lord, don't look on my sins and weaknesses. Honor the faith of this father, who wants his dead child brought back to life. Restore the soul of his son to his body, Lord."

As soon as Benedict finished his short, genuine request, the child's body began shaking and panting oddly. The closed eyes opened. Benedict took the child by the hand, pulled him to his feet, and gave him to his father. The father wept tears of joy then, hugging his once-dead son to him.

"Oh, my son! Father, thank you. Are you okay? Oh, Father! Son! Thank you, Father!"

"Don't thank me. Thank God. Now go and tell your wife."

And both the father and his son dashed home. Benedict retired to his cell to rest in prayers of thanksgiving.

CHAPTER 25

BENEDICT'S FINAL HEARTACHES

One of Benedict's best friends was a nobleman named Theoprobus. He had been converted to following Christ many years before by the Abbot's holy life and conversation. He visited Benedict often, and they talked about God and shared stories. One day as the cold winter weather was finally yielding to the promise of warmer days, Theoprobus arrived for his regular visit with his even-tempered friend Benedict, but was astounded to find him weeping bitterly in his cell, on his knees in prayer, his forehead pressed against the tiles of the floor.

What can be the matter? he wondered, as he rushed to his friend's side. Benedict did sometimes get sad about the unfairness of life or about a problem one of his sons had, but Theoprobus had never seen him sob uncontrollably like this. He also knew the Abbot usually preferred to stand before God in prayer. He bent down beside Benedict, putting his arm around his shoulders.

"Bennet, tell me. What's wrong, old friend?"

"Oh, Theoprobus. I'm glad you've come. But it's too terrible to speak of."

"Tell me. I'm listening. Here, I'll help you up."

So Benedict sat up on the floor. He began, red-eyed, "See this entire abbey?" He made a sweeping gesture with his right arm, taking in his cell and everything beyond it, including the monastery's outermost gardens and orchards.

"All this abbey. Every last stone in this place I've built with my brothers will—by God's omniscient decision—be given over to pagan invaders. To barbarians!

"But, Bennet. How do you know? Are you positive?"

"Yes, Theoprobus. Years from now. I saw. As I prayed, I saw. It will all be—" He closed his eyes and paused, as if he could not find the strength to continue. The horrors he had seen as he prayed had been too much.

When he found his voice again, he said, "Ruined. Crushed. Everything. Everything! Destroyed. Only barely did I win from God the promise my sons will be spared their precious lives. Oh, Theoprobus. We dug the rock for these very walls from the hard earth. We dug them up, boulder by boulder. Our hands raw with work. We ourselves. My family and I."

"But are you sure it will be . . . attacked?"

"Dead certain."

"Then God help us all, Bennet."

Benedict's prophecy came true. Some thirty years after his death, the Lombards destroyed Monte Cassino in the early 580s, and Benedict's monks fled to Rome, unharmed. The eighth-century Benedictine monk (and himself a Lombard), Paul the Deacon ("son of Warnefrid"), wrote of these

Lombard attacks in the fourth book of his *Historia gentis Langobardorum (History of the Lombard People):*

> About this time, the monastery of St. Benedict, which is situated on the hill of Casinum, was attacked at night by the Lombards. They plundered everything, but were unable to take any of the monks, so that the prophecy of the venerable Father Benedict, as seen by him years earlier, would be fulfilled. Also, the monks who fled from there made for Rome. They took with them the book of the holy Rule the Father had written, some other books, the weight for bread, the measure for wine, and what furniture they could transport.

These Lombards also destroyed the Subiaco monasteries and the one at Tarracina, devastating events foreseen by Benedict's meditating, prescient soul.

At the end of his war-pierced life, the white-haired Abbot was forced to acknowledge once again that only God holds the future. Because of this vision, the holy man knew his entire life's work would be overthrown at a distant, yet certain date, in a matter of a few hours by a ruthless gang. But Benedict did not give in to the potentially paralyzing threat of senseless future violence. He did not let it shake him from his present purpose. Though stunned, his faith in God never faltered. He turned to his friend Theoprobus, who was still watching him with concern.

"Theoprobus, what a world we live in," Benedict admitted.

His friend was too amazed to speak, but he lifted his friend to his feet and helped him sit on his cot. This small but pregnant gesture reminded the Abbot that there is strength in community, and that sometimes even those in leadership need an arm to lean on.

CHAPTER 26

CONVERSATION AND A CLOUD

Benedict's twin sister, Scholastica, was also in the habit of visiting her brother, although less frequently than Theoprobus, because she had her own sisters to shepherd at nearby Plumbariola. Once a year over countless years she had come to visit her beloved Benedict. Not long after Theoprobus' stay, Scholastica made her way with a few nuns to a small hut on the side of a mountain near Monte Cassino. Benedict also set out with a few monks and met her there with his usual warm hug. They refreshed their souls with the kind of transparent, untroubled conversation a person can only have with an intimate sibling. Later in the afternoon, food was brought to them, and only then did they remember they must eat.

As Benedict broke open a loaf of bread and handed Scholastica a piece, he observed, "Sister, it does my heart much good to see you, especially this year. We're not as strong as we once were, but the world's wars seem unabated." He looked away a moment, thinking of the gathering storm for Monte Cassino, before continuing, "But it gives me courage to see you, to know we're working together. I'm not alone. Our friendship brings me comfort. I thank God for you."

"Yes, and I for you, brother. I know what you mean. We talk and eat and all is peace. Conversation between us comes like white lace on spring cherry trees. Our friendship strengthens me. And yet, I grow old. I feel it. I'm weary of war. Of the world with fists. The women we see, grieving. Needy. Dead children. Missing husbands. Maimed limbs. The horrors never stop. And they're hungry. Nowhere to stay. I've seen children—well, you know—homeless, both parents gone. War orphans. The world is lost . . . to war. To its bitterness and pain. That's why I feel so old."

She looked out the window, where the evening light was thinning. "I don't want to leave you, Bennet. I'm comfortable here."

"I know. But we'll meet again, sister. We must go. Look at the shadows. It grows late. Our communities expect us back."

"Please, don't go. Not now. Not tonight. Stay with me and talk. Just stay."

"But Scholastica, you know it's the rule, and I'm the abbot. I can't be out all night. I must return to Monte Cassino. I'm sorry, sister. But I must."

"Just once? I'm not getting any younger, brother."

"Come now. We must both leave. You, too. We've plenty of time to return if we leave right now." He held out one hand to her, and with the other gestured for her to come. The disciplined monastic father in him was picturing the old gatekeeper Marcus waiting and wondering where he and the other monks accompanying him were. *He'll worry we've encountered a rockslide or a mountain lion or marauders. . . .*

But Scholastica did not take Benedict's proffered hand. She sat quietly at the dinner table, her head in her hands, as if she were praying. Her brother sat back down. "Scholastica? Scholastica?" He prodded her shoulder gently with his hand. "Are you all right?"

She did not speak. Instead, Gregory tells us that she lifted her head up as if listening for an answer from far off, and, the moment she lifted her head, tilting it slightly to one side, a crack of thunder split the air above them. Everyone in the hut jumped. Then they saw lightning dancing outside the windows of the simple shelter. The rain came down in sheets. The mountain ravines would soon flood. In a few short minutes, the way back would be rendered impassible. Only the most foolish would attempt a return journey up that mountain now.

"Sister! What have you done! Now I can't return, nor you."

Finally, Scholastica looked over at her brother, and she smiled softly, as if she was quite tired. When he saw that old familiar smile, he noticed suddenly, for the first time during their visit, how elderly his sister looked. He wondered if she was thinking the same about him as she watched him intently. He saw more wrinkles around her mouth and around her happy brown eyes. Her skin was looser on her arms and hands, her hair whiter. And he noticed she stooped more than she used to.

She must have seen something of this recognition in his face, for she reached over and patted his age-freckled hand gently. "Brother, I wanted you to stay. You wouldn't. I needed you to hear me. You didn't. So I asked God, couldn't you stay just this once. It seems our Lord answered my prayers with a resounding, 'Yes.' Don't you think?" She raised her eyebrows in question. "Can you stay with me awhile now?" She smiled again.

He smiled back and shrugged his shoulders. Taking her hand in both of his, he stayed up with her all night, and they talked through claps of thunder and bright lightning. No one in the little hut noticed these, though, because they were so focused on the conversation between Benedict and Scholastica, discussing the blessings of God: hot bread and beans, mountains and psalms, Nursia and Rome, humility and gardening, the simple joys of their childhood, as well as the complex responsibilities of guiding their monastic communities. No one slept that night.

When morning broke, the storm was spent, as was their final conversation. Scholastica rose and kissed her brother on the cheek. He teased her, asking, "So, now can I go?"

"Yes, but wasn't it good to be together, brother. I thank God for this time. I love you. I'm still sad to part, but at least I feel better about it now. God be with you and yours. Be careful. Stay safe. God bless you, sweet Bennet."

"And you, sister. God bless you, always." He sighed, "Now that we must part, I can't leave you. It feels different this time. It pinches here worse." He rubbed his thumb over his heart.

She reassured him with her old familiar smile, beginning in soft, dark eyes and ending in the upturned mouth. Through the singing of morning birds, they departed for the last time on earth, Benedict going back up to Monte Cassino, and Scholastica going down the mountain to her convent of Plumbariola.

CHAPTER 27

THE DEATH OF TWINS

Three days later, Benedict was standing in his cell at Monte Cassino, lifting his eyes up to heaven and praying early in the morning, when he saw the soul of his sister Scholastica leave her body and ascend like a dove into heaven. He knew his dearest friend was dead, gone from him to be with God. He rejoiced to see the glory of her journey from this world to the next, and went to tell his brothers the news. They gathered together and sang praises to almighty God on behalf of his sister.

Then Benedict sent to Plumbariola nunnery for Scholastica's body. En route, the monks met nuns from there coming to tell them the news of their abbess's death. They were surprised to learn the brothers already knew it. Then the monks and nuns returned together to the nunnery, and the Monte Cassino monks were given Scholastica's body to bring home to Benedict. Others readied the tomb that Benedict had fashioned for himself some time earlier, and they buried the abbess there in the oratory dedicated to St. John the Baptist. High and low came from near and far to attend the funeral of the compassionate sister who, like her brother, spent her life praising God by loving others in great detail.

Not long after his sister's death, Benedict was up before Vigils while his brothers were still in bed. His friend Abbot Servandus, who was visiting him, was sleeping in a room below his on the first floor. Standing and praying diligently in the dark hush of night, Benedict poured his soul out to God. Then he looked out his tower window to see a light so bright it illuminated everything in his vision. The holy man thought to himself, *It's brighter than daylight. Brighter even than the sun. Extraordinary. What incandescence!*

Then Benedict saw something else marvelous and strange. The whole world came into view, illumined by this miraculous light. In one giant beam of the most luminescent sun, he saw the entire radiant world. The Abbot watched indigo rivers, greenest meadows, purple mountains, and whitest clouds. He admired the crystal waters of snow-fed lakes and hills covered in olive groves and vineyards; he heard the cuckoos and nightingales of his childhood, then looked up to see stars and planets, asteroids and comets. He gazed down again and saw blue oceans and dolphins. Benedict found himself lost in this beauty. Once again, he praised God the Creator for the wonder of the earth.

He understood by the unique brightness of this vision that his own mortality was near. It reassured him that the path to heaven was both warm and well lit. Then he saw angels carrying the soul of Germanus, the Bishop of Capua, up to heaven in a fiery globe. Benedict wanted someone else to witness this miracle, so he called his friend Servandus, who was startled awake from a deep sleep when he heard, "Servandus, come! Look!"

Servandus worried that his friend Benedict was hurt. He leapt out of bed and ran up the stairs. By the time he got there, only a peculiar waning light remained. Benedict's words rushed out one after another, describing the shining vision to his friend. Then Benedict sent out a messenger to the city of Capua, to inquire after their Bishop Germanus, and the messenger returned to say Germanus had indeed died at the very moment Benedict had seen him ascending into heaven. The monks at Monte Cassino discussed this miracle and marveled at it.

Soon after this revelation, Benedict ordered his grave opened again. He told his monks he had six days more to live on earth. They cried and were filled with worry: "How can you be sure? Father, don't say that." They did not want him to go. They could not imagine life at Monte Cassino without kind Father Benedict.

He comforted them, saying, "But remember, God is with you, and I leave you my *Rule*. Study it. Live near God always. Pray and work. Always pray *and* work. Keep the balance in Christ."

Then Benedict contracted a raging fever and went to bed, sweating and faint. Every day his illness deepened, his fever slowly inching up. Then on the sixth day he asked his brothers to take him into the oratory of St. John the Baptist. They believed him then. They knew the end had come, and they carried him gently. Benedict received extreme unction there, taking and eating the body of Christ and drinking his blood for the last time on earth.

His disciples supported his weak body in the oratory so the holy man could stand at prayer one final time. Benedict lifted his hands to heaven, and his spirit left his earthly temple, ascending up into heaven after Scholastica and Germanus, along that path of light.

At this moment of transition, two monks had the same radiant vision, though they were in different locations. One was in his cell at Monte Cassino, the other on a trip far away. Both were praying, when they saw a bright road split the carbon sky all the way from Father Benedict's cell, stretching east, up to heaven. Covered by a rich, intricately patterned tapestry, this highway was hung with a thousand shining lamps. At the end of these lights, a man stood in a habit and demanded of them, "Do you know who's passing this way?"

Each of them answered, "No, I don't."

Then he said to them both, though they were in separate locations, "This is the way on which God's beloved servant Benedict is ascending into heaven. Watch and see."

The two monks who saw this vision ran to tell the others. That was how both the brothers present at Monte Cassino and those absent from the monastery learned of their father Benedict's death. Some have said this happened on the 21st of March, 547. Later, when the monks came together to celebrate Benedict's death, they reminded each other of his last words: "Be brave in God. Be peacemakers.

Read the *Rule*. Pray. Work. Be kind to each other. You're never alone. You've got each other. And God loves you. Blessings on you all, forever. Peace."

CHAPTER 28

A POSTHUMOUS TOUCH

One summer, many years later, a deeply troubled woman found herself wandering day and night, up and down and through the mountains and valleys and forests and fields near Benedict's cave in Subiaco. Like a strayed lamb, she was completely confused. Nothing was familiar. All of her life's usual emotional and physical signposts had vanished and, because of this, her mind had totally lost its bearings. She could no longer think logically. Once her best friend, analysis had become her greatest weakness and biggest foe.

Because she was anxious past the point of resolution, her body was exhausted from the stress of soul and mind. She eschewed eating, and never slept for long. She had forgotten what rest was and only stopped walking when her strength ran out. This was the sort of pause that cannot truly be called a "rest" but is more precisely known as a "break-down." Sometimes when her homeless, driven self was drained of energy and she lay down wherever she was at the moment, the prickly grass under her head and the sun-warm rocks against her back almost made her remember some words her mother had taught her many years before. But only fragments made it through the hot fog of her achy brain, like a drum beat, an incoherent repetition of "lie down . . . pastures . . . lie down . . . leads . . . green pastures . . . still . . . leads . . . lie down."

She closed her eyes and shook her head, then opened them without seeing anything and continued walking, swatting imaginary bees that threatened to sting her ears, as another refrain began to play over and over in her head, "Leads me . . . paths . . . name's sake . . . right . . . Leads me . . . paths . . . name's sake . . . right." The woman stumbled over knolls and digressed past lakes. At midday she found herself in front of a dark, cool gash in the landscape. She cocked her head and stared at it.

She had been wandering randomly, but she had not missed the right way, for this unremarkable-looking cave was Benedict's old home at Subiaco. Here the young hermit had spent three long years praying alone with God and cultivating the garden of his soul. This was where Benedict had learned about the mysterious, unending nature of God's kind, *agape* love. But this soul-sick woman did not know this. She did, however, understand she could lie in this inviting space and escape the summer heat and rains. She was also somehow drawn to its emotional warmth. She entered its blessed walls and slept there that night.

When this woman woke up in the morning, she stretched her stiff limbs, but was stopped in mid-stretch by birds singing. Immediately she was struck by the ability to hear herself think without its bringing pain. Something was running through her quiet head, clearly now. It sounded as sweet as the songs of birds to her:

The LORD is my shepherd, I shall not want. He makes me lie down in green pastures; he leads me beside still waters; he restores my soul. He leads me in right paths for his name's sake. Even though I walk through the darkest valley, I fear no evil; for you are with me; your rod and your staff—they comfort me. You prepare a table before me in the presence of my enemies; you anoint my head with oil; my cup overflows. Surely goodness and mercy shall follow me all the days of my life, and I shall dwell in the house of the LORD my whole life long.

"That's Psalm 23," she said aloud as she stepped out of the cave and into the bright sun. Then she took a deep breath and surveyed the alien landscape around her, her hands calmly on her hips. Her feet were unmoving but full of purpose. A wet thing like a diamond slipping down her cheek caught the bright light of morning. Finally, she sighted a hill she could recognize in the distance.

With one last grateful look back at the cave, she wiped the tear, felt the breeze dry its wetness on her thumb, and turned and began to run home. This woman who before had suffered from extreme mental illness was well the rest of her life. Her agitation turned to peace. Her confusion became clarity. Her worry became joy. Her self-focus became community. And her weakness became the strength of God.

This miracle showed the holy, healing power of Benedict, even after his death. Because he was God's friend, he left behind invisible strength and innumerable connections. To this day, the potent nature of his never-ending blessing is seen in the quiet muscle of his *Rule* and in the many Benedictines who wear his habit humbly, praying and working around the world for peace.

CHAPTER-BY-CHAPTER SUMMARY OF BENEDICT'S *RULE*

"A lamb can bathe in it without drowning, while an elephant can swim in it"; this ancient saying refers to a work of only seventy-three short chapters. Its wisdom is of two kinds: spiritual (how to live a Christocentric life on earth) and administrative (how to run a monastery efficiently). More than half of the chapters describe how to be obedient and humble, and what to do when a member of the community is not. About a fourth regulate the worship of God (the *Opus Dei*). A tenth outline how and by whom the monastery should be managed. And another tenth specifically describe the abbot's pastoral duties. In the summaries below, a modern, gender-inclusive version of Benedict's *Rule* is referenced.

PROLOGUE. Spiritually awake souls will seek out the twin duties of prayerful obedience and work, and their lives will be examples of holy listening, humility, and kindness. Anyone who is lazy spiritually is dangerously dozing, as Benedict stresses by quoting Romans 13:11: "[I]t is now the moment for you to wake from sleep."

CHAPTER 1. Benedict says his *Rule* is for the "bravest" of the four types of monks, the cenobites living in a monastery under an abbot. *(Cenobite* derives from the Greek *koinos* "common" and *bios* "life.")* Anchorites (or "hermits") live the solitary life; sarabaites live in twos and threes together, with no fixed rule; and gyrovagi wander "disreputably" from one monastery to another.

CHAPTER 2. The qualifications of an abbot or abbess are given as follows: They must correct those in their community with gentleness, and never prefer any brother or sister over another (leaders do not play favorites); they must also remember that the souls in their care are their responsibility (and from one to whom much is given, much will be required); and they must first make their own lives exemplary. ("Why do you see the speck in your neighbor's eye, but do not notice the log in your own eye?" Matthew 7:3).

CHAPTER 3. When decisions affecting the whole community must be decided, the *Rule* stipulates that the community come together in council to discuss these. The abbot or abbess must hear every view and then decide the matter, with the good of the community as their sole aim: "Do nothing without deliberation, but when you have acted, do not regret it" (Sirach 32:19).

CHAPTER 4. The necessities of obedience are found in following the Ten Commandments. Other spiritual guidelines are listed here: "Don't give way to anger," "Speak the truth," "Help the poor," "Clothe the naked," "Pray frequently,"

"Don't hate anyone," and, a Benedictine favorite, "Don't complain."

CHAPTER 5. Cheerful, prompt obedience to God and the superior is described as the first degree of humility. Benedict quotes the words of Jesus to the seventy disciples he appointed: "Whoever listens to you, listens to me" (Luke 10:16a).

CHAPTER 6. A moderate use of speech and much silence are recommended: "Death and life are in the power of the tongue" (Proverbs 18:21a).

CHAPTER 7. Humility and its twelve steps lead to the love of God.

CHAPTERS 8–19. Mindful participation in the Divine Office, the *Opus Dei,* is paramount ("nothing is to be preferred" above it). These "Canonical Hours" number seven during the day and one at night. Detailed arrangements are made for the number of psalms to be recited in winter and summer, on Sundays, weekdays, and Holy Days, and at other times. The main point of these chapters is "Sing wisely" (Psalm 47:7, "Sing praises with a psalm.") In other words, sing as a way of concentrating your soul on God.

CHAPTER 20. This chapter is all about prayer. It points out that if we approach someone powerful on earth with reverence when we want to ask them something, with how much more humility should we approach God? Also, brevity in praying is encouraged. God is said to look at the purity of our hearts, not at the number of our words. The *Rule* especially points out that the best communal prayers are "brief."

CHAPTER 21. The appointment of monastic deans is outlined.

CHAPTER 22. This chapter describes how the monastic members are to sleep. They must retire in their habits, for example, so they are always ready to rise for prayer and work. A candle must be kept burning all night, and the beds of younger monks or nuns should be interspersed among those of the older brothers and sisters.

CHAPTERS 23–30. These chapters deal with offenses against the *Rule* and against community, with a graduated scale of penalties: "Those who are well have no need of a physician, but those who are sick" (Matthew 9:12).

CHAPTER 31. How to appoint a cellarer is addressed in this chapter. He must be "wise, of mature character, sober, not a great eater, not haughty, not excitable, not offensive, not slow, not wasteful, but a God-fearing man." If this cellarer discovers a shortage of any supply, he or she is instructed to share this bad news with the community gently: "Indeed, does not a [kind] word surpass a good gift?" (Sirach 18:17).

CHAPTER 32. This brief chapter outlines the proper care of the monastery's valuable tools and goods. With much common sense, it instructs the brothers and sisters to handle the ordinary garden tools and kitchen implements as lovingly and as respectfully as the sacred vessels of God's altar. All of life requires respect.

CHAPTER 33. Private ownership is forbidden to those in monastic orders.

CHAPTER 34. Possessions must be shared according to the needs and infirmities of each community member. Complaining is strictly forbidden.

CHAPTER 35. All community members are ordered to take turns serving in the kitchen.

CHAPTERS 36-37. This section outlines the care of the sick, the old, and the young, especially in relaxing the *Rule* for them in matters of food: "I was sick and you took care of me" (Matthew 25:36).

CHAPTER 38. This chapter describes the weekly edification through communal reading during meals.

CHAPTERS 39–41. These regulate monastic food and drink. Two meals a day are recommended, with two (or three) dishes of cooked food at each. Also, each brother or sister is allowed a pound of bread and about half a pint of wine. Meat is given only to the sick and the weak. Mealtime(s) vary with the seasons of the year.

CHAPTER 42. This section forbids speaking after Compline.

CHAPTER 43. This chapter discusses how to deal with the vice of tardiness, especially for those who come late to prayer or meals.

CHAPTERS 44–46. Confession is essential to the community. Mistakes must be acknowledged and forgiven. These chapters also outline punishments for wrongdoing.

CHAPTER 47. Here is described how the abbot is to call his community to the *Opus Dei.*

CHAPTER 48. "Idleness is the enemy of the soul"; this chapter stresses the significance of both manual labor and sacred reading, and arranges times to be devoted to these daily.

CHAPTER 49. This chapter describes how to observe Lent.

CHAPTERS 50-51. Monks or nuns who work in the fields or travel must stay in touch with their home community as much as possible, and, if they cannot make it back to the monastery in time, they must pray wherever they are.

CHAPTER 52. This chapter restricts the use of the oratory. It is for devotional purposes only (and is not to be used for storage).

CHAPTER 53. Each guest must be treated like Christ: "I was a stranger and you welcomed me" (Matthew 25:35). Kind hospitality is the "bread and butter" of Benedictines.

CHAPTER 54. Monks and nuns are forbidden to receive letters or gifts without the superior's permission.

CHAPTER 55. Those in the monastic community should dress as modestly and as inexpensively as possible, and old habits are to be given to the poor. Monks and nuns should also use the simplest bedding.

CHAPTER 56. Guests are to eat at the abbot's or abbess's table.

CHAPTER 57. The artists of the monastery must be humble and price their crafts below the usual trading value, and they must never defraud anyone.

CHAPTER 58. This chapter describes how new members will be admitted. The potential new member first spends time in the community as a guest; then he or she is admitted to the novitiate under the care of a novice-master (and is free to leave during this time). Next, if after a twelve-month probation the novice still desires to join the community, they take the vows of stability, conversion of life, and obedience, binding them for life to the monastery of their profession, in that location. Benedictines are careful to dedicate themselves to Christ and also to a particular place, to work there, pray there, and give stability to that locale and all its people. This *stabilitas loci* allows each monastic community to grow its special family spirit.

CHAPTER 59. This chapter describes the admission of children to the community.

CHAPTERS 60, 62. These chapters regulate the admission of priests to the community. They are told to set an example of humility to all. They are allowed to exercise their priestly functions only by permission of the superior.

CHAPTER 61. This chapter describes the reception of monastic brothers and sisters from outside the community and how to admit them if they wish to join the community.

CHAPTER 63. Respectful behavior makes community possible. The young are to honor their elders, and the senior members to respect and love the young. All honor the abbot or abbess as Christ's representative, and the superior, in turn, must be impartial and kind to all.

CHAPTER 64. This chapter outlines how to elect the abbot or abbess. This leader must not be "excitable, anxious, extreme, obstinate, jealous, or over suspicious."

CHAPTER 65. Here is regulated how to appoint a prior, if needed, and warns the prior not to be puffed up with iniquitous pride.

CHAPTER 66. This chapter describes how to appoint a porter. The porter must be old, wise, and dependable, not given to straying from the key post of answering the door. Above all, the porter is charitable: "As soon as anyone knocks or a poor person calls on the monastery, let the porter answer, 'Thanks be to God,' or invoke a blessing."

CHAPTER 67. Monastic members are told how to behave when they travel.

CHAPTER 68. All orders must be obeyed cheerfully, no matter how difficult they seem.

CHAPTER 69. This chapter forbids monastic members from defending each other.

CHAPTER 70. Members of the community are prohibited from striking another.

CHAPTER 71. This chapter encourages general obedience and explains that the obstinate must be punished.

CHAPTER 72. Generosity and true charity must become a way of living: "[L]ove one another with mutual affection; outdo one another in showing honor" (Romans 12:10). The members of the monastic community must be patient with each other's flaws, serve each other, love God and their superiors humbly, and prefer nothing whatever to Christ.

CHAPTER 73. In the epilogue, Benedict declares his *Rule* imperfect. It is not the last word, he says, but a few words about the Word. This guideline to godliness is written primarily for all who consider themselves beginners spiritually, because, with God's help, he reminds, anything is possible (see Philippians 4:13).

PREVIOUS POPES WITH THE REGNAL NAME "BENEDICT" ("BLESSED")

In addition to the current Roman pontiff, Pope Benedict XVI, "Benedict" has been the regnal name of fourteen other popes. This appendix lists them from contemporary times back to Benedict I (575–579). Most headed the Catholic Church in the Middle Ages. Antipopes with this name are not listed below. These antipopes include Benedict X, XIII, and two XIV's, whose claim to the papacy was the result of a disputed election.

POPE BENEDICT XVI (2005–present)
On April 16, 1927, Joseph Alois Ratzinger was born into a volatile world, the *Götterdämerung* of the Weimar Republic. He arrived on a bitterly cold Holy Saturday in the small Bavarian village of Marktl am Inn, today about 3,000 residents. The 265th pope says he chose "Benedict" because he wants to continue the legacies of Pope Benedict XV's inclusive, humanitarian diplomacy and balanced opposition to modernism, as well as St. Benedict's emphasis on humility and intimacy with God. Pope Benedict XVI was preceded by Pope John Paul II.

BENEDICT XV (1914–1922)
Giacomo della Chiesa was born on November 21, 1854, to a noble Italian family in Pegli. He studied law at the Royal

University of Genoa and theology at Rome's Gregorian University. Ordained to the priesthood in 1878, he earned a doctorate in sacred theology the next year. Giacomo entered the papal diplomatic service in 1882. He served as secretary to the nuncio to Spain until 1887 and as secretary to the Vatican Secretary of State until 1901. Della Chiesa negotiated a resolution in Germany and Spain's dispute over the Caroline Islands. He also organized relief during a cholera epidemic. In 1907, he became Archbishop of Bologna and in May 1914 was ordained a cardinal. Benedict XV was elected on September 3, 1914, a month after World War I broke out. He took a neutral stand and worked to mitigate the suffering of war victims. He tried to broker peace, but failed. Both sides regarded his pacifistic stance as a cover for support for the other side in a war he condemned as "the suicide of Europe." After the war, he asked that the Vatican be included in the Paris Peace Conference, but was refused. He petitioned the victorious Allies to lift the blockade against Germany and alleviate the suffering it was causing women and children. He also took up a Church-wide collection to buy food. A small, often sick man, he is mostly remembered for his generosity and humane leadership during World War I. Pope Benedict XV was 67 when he died of influenza on January 22, 1922. His predecessor was Pius X, and he was succeeded by Pius XI.

BENEDICT XIV (1740–1758)

Prospero Lorenzo Lambertini was born to a noble family in Bologna on March 31, 1675. At that time, Bologna was the second largest city in the Papal States. His election came at a very difficult time for the papacy because of disputes between it and the Roman Catholic nations, but he managed to settle these with the Kingdoms of Naples, Sardinia, Spain, Venice, and Austria. About his potential election as Pope, he reputedly commented, "If you want to elect a saint, choose Gotti; if you want a statesman, take Aldrovandi; if you want an honest man, pick me." His papacy was industrious. He championed reform in the education of priests, in the calendar of ecclesiastical feasts, and in many papal institutions. He denounced the use of Christian words and terms to represent non-Christian ideas and cultural traditions, an accommodation made by the Jesuits in their Indian and Chinese missions. With Cardinal Passionei, he also began the Vatican Library catalog. This Pope Benedict had a reputation for intelligence and conciliation. During his reign, the Catholic Church was frequently criticized by Enlightenment scholars, but Pope Benedict XIV supported scientific learning and encouraged restraint in selecting publications for the *Index Librorum Prohibitorum* (Index of Forbidden Books). In an odd twist of history, the French writer and philosopher Voltaire dedicated his tragedy *Mahomet* to Benedict XIV. Benedict XIV was preceded by Clement XII and succeeded by Clement XIII.

BENEDICT XIII (1724–1730)
Pietro Francesco Orsini was born on February 2, 1649, in Gravina di Puglia, Italy. He was the last member of the

great Orsini family of Rome to become pope. His election, however, was not easy. In May of 1724, two months into the meeting to elect the next pope, the conclave began to favor Orsini, but he was not receptive. He tried instead to prevent his election to the papacy, and, once chosen, Orsini refused to capitulate until his colleagues convinced him it would be impossibly difficult to reconvene the conclave and re-vote. At first he called himself Benedict XIV (because of the superstition that the number thirteen brings bad luck), but later he accepted "Benedict XIII" as his title. He was a reforming pope, working to halt the licentious living of the Italian priests and cardinals. As pope, Benedict XIII was noted for his scholarly pursuits and for living a deliberately simple life. He also did not engage in worldly politics. Benedict XIII was preceded by Innocent XIII and succeeded by Clement XII.

BENEDICT XII (1334–1342)

Jacques Fournier was born in Saverdun in the Comté de Foix sometime in the 1280s. Scant information exists about this pope's modest origins and boyhood in southern France. A rotund Cistercian monk, he studied at the University of Paris. In 1311, he was made Abbot of Fontfroide. He had a reputation for intelligence and obsessive organizational skills. Ordained Bishop of Pamiers in 1317, he ordered a witch hunt for the Cathar heretics, celibate vegetarians who believed in reincarnation and called the Church of Rome "a den of thieves." In 1326, when the last Cathars in southern France were said to have been extirpated,

Fournier was made Bishop of Mirepoix. A year later, he became a cardinal.

Although Benedict XII is known as a reforming pope who preached against and worked to eradicate ecclesiastical greed, the medieval landscape was overrun at this time by indulgence-selling pardoners and rich friars, corruption parodied famously by Chaucer (1343–1400) in his *Canterbury Tales*. Benedict XII ordered the construction of an opulent papal palace in Avignon and spent much of his time contemplating questions of theology, debating scholastic theology with William of Ockham and Meister Eckhart, and rejecting many of the ideas developed by Pope John XXII. Benedict XII also campaigned against the Immaculate Conception. The third pope to reside at Avignon during the Avignon papacy (1305–1378), Benedict XII saw the beginning of the Hundred Years' War in 1336. He was preceded by John XXII and succeeded by Clement VI.

BENEDICT XI (1303-1304)
Nicholas Boccasini was born in Treviso, Italy, in 1240. At fourteen, he entered the Dominican order, and fourteen years later, he became a lector of theology. He was made Master General of the order in 1296 and was unanimously elected to the papacy in October of 1303, but died eight months later in July of 1304. He may have been poisoned. Most of his short eight-month reign handled the aftermath of Pope Boniface VIII's unlawful arrest by Philip IV of France, and the main accomplishment of his pontificate

was the restoration of peace with the French court. Benedict XI authored a volume of sermons and commentaries on the Gospel of Matthew, the Psalms, the Book of Job, and Revelation. His successors were dominated by French kings and relocated the papal seat from Rome to Avignon. This Avignon papacy is also known as the Babylonian Captivity. Beatified in 1773, Benedict XI was preceded by Boniface VIII and succeeded by Clement V.

BENEDICT IX (1032–1044, 1045, 1047-1048)

Theophylactus was born around 1012 and held the papacy for three non-consecutive reigns. The nephew of both Pope Benedict VIII and Pope John XIX, he was the last of the popes from the powerful Tusculani family. In October 1032, his father, Alberich III, count of Tusculum, imposed Benedict IX on the chair at about age twenty, making him one of the youngest popes in history.

His first reign was violent and debauched, and when the Romans revolted, the pope fled for his life. Silvester III was elected in 1044 but was driven out by Benedict's brothers a year later. Benedict IX did not remain pope long this second time. Some suspect he wanted to marry, because he sold the papacy for some 1450 pounds of gold (650 kilograms) to his priest godfather, John Gratian, who became Gregory VI. Apparently Benedict changed his mind not long after, for he returned to Rome to reclaim the papacy at the same time Silvester III returned to Rome to make the same claim. Henry III of Germany stepped in and deposed all three popes, and Clement II was made pope. When Clement died,

Benedict returned one last time and installed himself as pope in November of 1047. He lasted only eight months before Henry ordered him out. He was never seen in Rome again. He may have become a penitent at Grottaferrata until his death in 1055 or 1056.

In Benedict IX's first reign, he was preceded by John XIX and succeeded by Silvester III; in his second reign, he was preceded by Silvester III and succeeded by Gregory VI; and in his third and last reign, he was preceded by Clement II and succeeded by Damasus II. He has been called "a disgrace" to the papacy.

BENEDICT VIII (1012–1024)

Benedict VIII is the first of several popes from the powerful Tusculani family. A layman, he was imposed on the papal chair, but despite this less-than-democratic start, he was considered a powerful, and, by most accounts, a good pope. In 1014, he crowned Henry II of Germany Holy Roman Emperor. Benedict VIII fought simony, and in the 1022 synod of Pavia, he supported the Clunian reform of a lax clergy. His date of birth is unknown. He was preceded by Sergius IV and was succeeded by his brother John XIX.

BENEDICT VII (974–983)

The Roman faction that killed Benedict VI also made trouble for the seventh Benedict. When this faction it put the antipope Boniface VII on the throne, Emperor Otto II sent Count Sicco to sort out this problem. Boniface was expelled, an election was held, and Benedict VII was made pope. Benedict VII worked to stunt the growth of simony in the Church, while he supported the advancement of monasteries and learning. He governed Rome quietly for nearly nine years. Benedict's date of birth is not known with certainty. In September 981, he convened a Lateran Synod. Preceded by Benedict VI, he was succeeded by John XIV (who in turn was murdered by Boniface VII in 984).

BENEDICT VI (973-974)

Chosen with great ceremony and installed as pope under the protection of the Emperor Otto the Great, Benedict VI reigned for a brief period that was remarkable only for its inauspicious end. Imprisoned in the Castle of Sant'Angelo by a faction of the Roman nobility, Benedict VI was strangled some two months later by order of Crescentius, the son of the infamous Theodora. He was preceded by John XIII and was succeeded by Benedict VII.

BENEDICT V (MAY TO JUNE 964)

The learned Benedict V was known as "Grammaticus." After Emperor Otto I deposed John XII and installed Leo VIII on the papal throne, the Romans expelled Leo VIII, and, after John XII died, they elected Benedict V; however, soon after, Benedict was degraded to deacon and brought back to Hamburg with Otto, where he spent his last year. He died in July of 965. At the synod that deposed him, the pastoral staff was broken over his head by Leo VIII. Preceded by Leo VIII, he was succeeded by John XIII.

BENEDICT IV (900–903)

Owing to the sketchy nature of tenth-century papal records, very little is known about this fourth Benedict, who was the son of Mammalus, a native of Rome. We do know that he became pope when John IX died, that he crowned Louis the Blind as Holy Roman Emperor, and that he excommunicated Baldwin II of Flanders for having Archbishop Fulk of Rheims murdered. Benedict IV died the summer of 903 and was buried by the gate of Guido in front of St. Peter's. He was preceded by John IX and succeeded by Leo V.

BENEDICT III (855–858)

Controversy surrounded the election of this learned Roman ascetic. After the death of Leo IV in July of 855, some influential legates for Benedict III suddenly threw their support behind Anastasius the Librarian, with the result that Benedict was jailed. Eventually, however, popular opinion prevailed, and his election was confirmed. Benedict III may have met the future king of Wessex, Alfred the Great (born 849, ruled 871–899) when the prince visited Rome with his father, King Æthelwulf (839–856). Envoys of Emperor Louis II required Benedict to treat Anastasius and his followers with clemency. The schism weakened the power of emperors to influence the election of popes. He was preceded by Leo IV and succeeded by Nicholas I.

BENEDICT II (684-685)

Also a Roman, the second Benedict was famous for his singing and for his deep knowledge of Scripture. After Leo II died in June of 683 and Benedict II was elected, it took nearly a year for the new pope to be confirmed by Emperor Constantine Pogonatus. As pope, he worked hard to combat Monothelitism, a seventh-century Byzantine heresy proposing that Jesus Christ has two natures (human and divine) but only one, divine will. It denied the human will of Christ. Benedict II was preceded by Leo II, and he was succeeded by John V.

BENEDICT I (575–579)

Almost nothing is known about the first Pope Benedict. He was a Roman and the son of Boniface, and assumed the papacy some twenty to thirty years after Benedict of Nursia's death. The brutal Lombard invasions of Italy delayed by almost a year Benedict's confirmation by Emperor Justin II. (John III died in July of 574, and Benedict I was installed in June of 575.) His pontificate saw four hard years of famine and plague in the aftermath of the Lombard invasions in Italy, and the *Liber Pontificalis* (*Book of Popes*) says Benedict I died in the middle of dealing with these problems. He may have chosen the regnal name "Benedict" as a conscious effort to follow in the footsteps of one who worked to establish peace and to feed the poor. He was buried in the vestibule of the sacristy of the old basilica of St. Peter. Benedict I was preceded by John III, and he was succeeded by Pelagius II.

NOTES

1. Odo John Zimmerman, translator, *St. Gregory the Great: Dialogues* (Washington, D.C.: Catholic University of America Press, 2002), 3-4.

2. This is my translation. See also Leo Sherley-Price and D. H. Farmer, translators, *Bede: Ecclesiastical History of the English People with Bede's Letter to Egbert and Cuthbert's Letter on the Death of Bede* (NY: Penguin Books, 1990), 73.

3. Robert C. Gregg, *Athanasius: The Life of Antony and the Letter to Marcellinus* (Mahwah, NJ: Paulist Press, Inc., 1980), 125.

4. Gregg, 145, 109.

5. Odo John Zimmerman and Benedict R. Avery, translators, *Gregory the Great: Life and Miracles of St. Benedict* (Book II, *Dialogues*) (Westport, CT: Greenwood Press, 1980), iv.

6. Ildephonso Schuster, *Saint Benedict and His Times* (London: B. Herder, 1951), 2.

7. Deborah Mauskopf Deliyannis, editor, *Historiography in the Middle Ages* (Boston: Brill, 2003), 1-2.

8. G. R. Evans, *The Thought of Gregory the Great* (Cambridge: Cambridge University Press, 1986), 47-48.

9. This is my translation. See also Sherley-Price, 93.

10. Henry Davis, translator, *St. Gregory the Great: Pastoral Care* (NY: Newman Press, 1978), 56.

11. Davis, 89-90.

12. Davis, 90-91.

13. The excerpts that follow are from Sherley-Price and Farmer, at pages 72 ff. See also the Bertram Colgrave entry in the Recommended Further Reading List.

14. Ewert Cousins, translator, *Bonaventure: The Soul's Journey into God, The Tree of Life, The Life of St. Francis* (NY: Paulist Press, 1978), 260.

15. This is my translation. See also Brian Tierney, *The Middle Ages* (NY: Alfred A. Knopf, Inc., 1983), 45.

16. This is my translation. See also Tierney, 93.

17. Mayeul de Dreuille, *The Rule of St. Benedict: A Commentary in Light of World Ascetic Traditions* (NY: Paulist Press, 2002), 57-58.

18. de Dreuille, 122.

19. Michael Grant, editor, *Latin Literature: An Anthology* (NY: Penguin Books, 1967), 139, 184-185.

20. Grant, 185.

21. Grant, 266.

22. Grant, 291-292.

23. James J. O'Donnell, *Cassiodorus* (Berkeley: University of California Press, 1979), Chapter 6.

24. J. S. Watson, translator, *Cicero on Oratory and Orators* (NY: Harper and Brothers, 1875), 274-275.

25. Roy J. Deferrari, translator, *Saint Basil: The letters* (4 volumes) (Cambridge, MA: Harvard University Press, 1970–1988), volume 1, xxii.

26. This is my translation. See also de Dreuille, 114.

27. This is my translation. See also Raymond Canning, translator, *The Rule of St. Augustine* (Garden City, NY: Image Books, 1986), 11.

28. This is my translation. See also Basil Davenport, editor, *The Portable Roman Reader* (NY: Penguin Books, 1979), 603.

29. Grant, 51.

30. John 15:19.

31. Grant, 373.

32. Thomas J. Heffernan, "Christian Biography: Foundation to Maturity" in *Historiography in the Middle Ages*, ed. Deborah Mauskopf Deliyannis, 145-146 (Boston: Brill, 2003).

33. Grant, 399-400.

34. This is my translation. See also Grant, 398.

35. Grant, 422.

36. Davenport, 652.

37. Matthew 3:1-3.

38. G. A. Loud, "Monastic Chronicles in the Twelfth-Century Abruzzi" in *Anglo-Norman Studies XXVII*, ed. John Gillingham, 117 (Woodbridge, Suffolk: Boydell Press, 2005).

39. Grant, 310.

40. This is my translation. See also Abbot Justin McCann, OSB, *Saint Benedict* (London: Sheed and Ward, Ltd., 1979), 69.

41. This is my translation. See also Paul Halsall, editor, *Internet Medieval Sourcebook* (NY: Fordham University Center for Medieval Studies), September 1998, http://www.fordham.edu/halsall/basis/palladius-lausiac.html (accessed September 10, 2005). Chapter 28, paragraph 26.

42. 1 Corinthians 2:9.

43. Psalm 11:71.

RECOMMENDED FURTHER READING LIST

Readers who want to explore St. Benedict further can check out these recommended books (selected from the mountains of those available). The annotated list includes historical scholarship, as well as translations of and commentaries on Benedict's *Rule*.

Bangley, Bernard and Fr. Alban Butler. *Butler's Lives of the Saints*. Concise, modernized edition. Brewster, MA: Paraclete Press, 2005. First published from 1756–1759. Widely read through four centuries (in various revised editions).

Barry, Patrick, OSB. *St. Benedict's Rule: A New Translation for Today*. Hidden Spring, 2004. Features inclusive, contemporary language and a streamlined text.

Bradley, Guy. *Ancient Umbria: State, Culture, and Identity in Central Italy from the Iron Age to the Augustan Era*. Oxford: Oxford University Press, 2000. Fills a critical lacuna.

Brown, Peter. *The World of Late Antiquity, AD 150–750*. NY: W. W. Norton, 1971. A good overview.

Canham, Elizabeth. *Heart Whispers: Benedictine Wisdom for Today*. Nashville: Upper Room Books, 1999. Explains how the *Rule*'s spiritual guidelines can be lived out today. Popular with women's study groups.

Canning, Raymond, OSA, trans. *The Rule of St. Augustine*. Introduction and commentary by Tarsicius J. van Bavel, OSA Garden City, NY: Image Books, 1986. Includes both masculine and feminine versions, plus plain-speaking commentary.

Chesterton, G. K. *Life of Saint Francis*. 1924. Garden City, NY: Image Books, 2001. Inimitable life of St. Francis by the well-known, twentieth-century writer.

Chittister, Joan, OSB. *The Rule of Benedict: Insights for the Ages*. New York: Crossroad Publishing Company, 1992. Fine contemporary commentary on St. Benedict's *Rule* by a prominent teacher and speaker.

Colgrave, Bertram, ed. and trans. *The Earliest Life of Gregory the Great by an Anonymous Monk of Whitby*. Cambridge: Cambridge University Press, 1985. Presents the story of Gregory's puns in chapter 9.

Cornell, Tim. *The Beginnings of Rome: Italy and Rome from the Bronze age to the Punic*. London: Routledge, 1995. A readable Roman history.

Cousins, Ewert, trans. and intro. *Bonaventure: The Soul's Journey into God, The Tree of Life, The Life of St. Francis*. NY: Paulist Press, 1978. A sturdy translation.

Davenport, Basil, ed. *The Portable Roman Reader*. NY: Penguin Books, 1979. A good compendium of Roman writings.

Davis, Henry, SJ, trans. *St. Gregory the Great: Pastoral Care*. NY: Newman Press, 1978. A splendid translation of this classic explication of pastoral duties.

Deferrari, Roy J., trans. *Saint Basil: The Letters*. 4 vols. Cambridge, MA: Harvard University Press, 1970–1988. Solid translations of one of St. Benedict's greatest inspirations and sources.

Deliyannis, Deborah Mauskopf, ed. *Historiography in the Middle Ages*. Boston: Brill, 2003. A valuable collection of essays.

Doyle, Leonard J., trans. *The Rule of St. Benedict*. Collegeville, MN.: The Liturgical Press, 2001. A fine masculine version, one of the most widely used English translations of the *Rule*. Appearing in 1948, has remained in print ever since.

de Dreuille, Mayeul, OSB. *The Rule of St. Benedict: A Commentary in Light of World Ascetic Traditions*. New York: Paulist Press, 2002. An intelligent text putting the *Rule* into a global context.

Eberle, Luke and Charles Philippi, trans. *The Rule of the Master*. Kalamazoo, MI: Cistercian Publications, 1977. First English translation of the Italian RM.

Engs, Ruth Clifford. "St. Scholastica: Finding Meaning in Her Story." St. Meinrad, IN: Abby Press, 2003. http://www.indiana.edu/~engs/scholas.htm. Scholarly article presenting the scant facts about Scholastica, as we know them.

Evans, G. R. *The Thought of Gregory the Great.* Cambridge Studies in Medieval Life and Thought: Fourth Series. Cambridge: Cambridge University Press, 1986. A quotation-studded overview of this patristic father's seminal thought.

Fletcher, Richard. *The Barbarian Conversion: From Paganism to Christianity.* NY: Henry Holt and Company, Inc., 1997. A sharp history by an Oxbridge scholar.

Fremantle, Anne. *A Treasury of Early Christianity.* NY: Viking Press, 1960. Slender volume packed with classic texts.

Fry, Timothy, OSB, ed. *RB1980: The Rule of St. Benedict in English: In Latin and English with Notes.* Collegeville, MN: The Liturgical Press, 1981. Often referred to by the shorthand "RB80" or "RB1980," the standard masculine version.

Galbraith, Craig S. and Oliver Galbraith, III. *The Benedictine Rule of Leadership: Classic Management Secrets You Can Use Today.* Avon, MA: Adams Media Corporation, 2004. Examination of the Benedictine way as applied to the administration of corporations, with an emphasis on true community-building and accountability.

Grant, Michael, ed. *Latin Literature: An Anthology.* NY: Penguin Books, 1967. The best translations (by John Dryden, Alexander Pope, Samuel Johnson, and others).

Gregg, Robert C. *Athanasius: The Life of Antony and the Letter to Marcellinus.* Mahwah, NJ: Paulist Press, Inc., 1980. A splendid rendering of this ancient life.

Gregory the Great. *The Life of St. Benedict* (Book II, *Dialogues*). Hilary Costello and Eoin de Bhaldraithe, trans. Commentary by Adalbert de Vogüé, OSB, Petersham: St. Bede's Publications, 1993. Solid and useful.

―――. *Life and Miracles of St. Benedict* (Book II, *Dialogues*). A translation of this classic source, sponsored by the Order of St. Benedict, found on-line at http://www.osb.org/gen/greg (adapted for hypertext by Bro. Richard, July 2001).

―――. *Patrologia Latina*. Ed. Jacques-Paul Migne. Volumes 75–79. Paris: Imprimerie Catholique, 1841–1864. Nineteenth-century Latin texts of Gregory's oeuvre, *Dialogues* Book Two (found in volume 66). Also on-line at http://www.proquest.co.uk/products/pld.html. Twentieth-century editions of these found in *Corpus Christianorum, Series Latina*. Volumes 140–144. Turnhout, Belgium: Typographi Brepols, 1953.

Halsall, Paul, ed. *Internet Medieval Sourcebook*. NY: Fordham University Center for Medieval Studies. http://www.fordham.edu/halsall/basis/palladius-lausiac.html. Superb Jesuit-sponsored Internet source. September 1998 (accessed September 10, 2005).

Hart, Basil Henry Liddell Hart. *The Other Side of the Hill: Germany's generals, their rise and fall, with their own account of military events, 1939–1945*. NY: Cassell, 1973. Historical text providing soldiers' accounts of Monte Cassino bombing.

Heffernan, Thomas J. "Christian Biography: Foundation to Maturity." In *Historiography in the Middle Ages*. ed. Deborah Mauskopf Deliyannis. Boston: Brill, 2003. 115–154. Very readable scholarly article on Gregory's historical milieu.

Hodgkin, Thomas. *Italy and Her Invaders*. Eight volumes. Oxford: Clarendon Press, 1892–1899. By historian, archaeologist, and chronicler trying to supplement Edward Gibbon's work.

Holmes, Augustine. *A Life Pleasing to God: The Spirituality of the Rules of St. Basil*. Kalamazoo, MI: Cistercian Publications, 2000. Well-researched.

Holmes, George, ed. *The Oxford History of Medieval Europe*. Oxford: Oxford University Press, 1992. Helpful collection of essays and maps on medieval Europe.

Johnston, Harold. *The Private Life of the Romans*. NY: Cooper Square Publishers, 1973. Describes the day-to-day life of Romans.

Kardong, Terrence G., OSB. *Benedict's Rule: A Translation and Commentary*. Collegeville, MN: The Liturgical Press, 1996. First English-language line-exegesis of the complete *Rule*, with keen commentary.

Keen, Maurusice. *Medieval Warfare: A history*. Oxford: Oxford University Press, 1999. Essential to understanding war in the Middle Ages.

Lawrence, C. H. *Medieval Monasticism: Forms of religious life in Western Europe in the Middle Ages*. 2nd edition.

London: Longman, 1989. A splendid historical overview.

Loud, G. A. "Monastic Chronicles in the Twelfth-Century Abruzzi." In *Anglo-Norman Studies XXVII: Proceedings of the Battle Conference 2004.* ed. John Gillingham. Woodbridge, Suffolk: Boydell Press, 2005. 101–131.

Markus, R. A. *Gregory the Great and His World.* Cambridge: Cambridge University Press, 1997. A study dealing with the major contributions made by Gregory's mission-minded papacy.

McCann, Justin, OSB. *Saint Benedict.* London: Sheed and Ward, Ltd., 1979. A worthwhile life of this saint, written by a twentieth-century monk and Oxford-educated classics teacher.

Meyer, Robert T., trans. *Palladius: The Lausiac History.* London: Longmans, Green and Co., 1965. Compare Halsall. A good translation.

Mork, Wulstan, OSB. *The Benedictine Way.* Petersham: St. Bede's Publications, 1987. Good background information on the Benedictines.

O'Donnell, James J. *Cassiodorus.* Berkeley: University of California Press, 1979. A much-consulted work on ancient scholarship now found on-line at http://history medren.about.com/gi/dynamic/offsite.htm?site=http://ccat. sas.upenn.edu/%7Ejod/texts/cassbook/toc.html.

O'Donovan, Patrick. *Benedict of Nursia*. New York: HarperCollins Publishers, 1984. Enjoyable life of St. Benedict.

Order of St. Benedict. *The Rule of St. Benedict: An index to texts on-line and gateway to RB Bibliographic Index*. Collegeville, MN: St. John's Abbey. http:// www.osb.org /rb/index.html#English. Web site with handy multi-lingual translations and bibliographic information on the *Rule*.

Rippinger, Joel, OSB. *The Benedictine Order in the United States: An Interpretive History*. Collegeville, MN: The Liturgical Press, 1990. A modern look at the life and work of this ancient Christian order.

Robinson, David. *The Family Cloister: Benedictine Wisdom for the Home*. New York: Crossroad, 2000. Written for parents.

Schuster, Ildephonso. *Saint Benedict and His Times*. Gregory J. Roettger, trans. London: B. Herder, 1951. Helps re-create Benedict's cultural and historical milieu.

Sherley-Price, Leo, and D. H. Farmer, trans. *Bede: Ecclesiastical History of the English People with Bede's Letter to Egbert and Cuthbert's Letter on the Death of Bede*. Revised by R. E. Latham. NY: Penguin Books, 1990. Reliable translation of Bede.

Silvas, Anna. *Asketikon of St. Basil the Great*. Oxford: Oxford University Press, 2005. A new English translation and treatment of the emergence of monasticism in Asia Minor.

Straw, Carole. *Gregory the Great*. Berkeley: University of California Press, 1991. Presents Gregory as a complex and profoundly human saint.

Tierney, Brian. *The Middle Ages: Volume I, Sources of Medieval History*. NY: Alfred A. Knopf, Inc., 1983. A concise compendium of major medieval sources.

Van Deusen, Nancy E., ed. *The Place of the Psalms in the Intellectual Culture of the Middle Ages*. NY: SUNY Press, 1999. Profound historical analysis of the Psalms and their ubiquitous importance in medieval culture.

de Waal, Esther. *A Life-Giving Way: A Commentary on the Rule of St. Benedict*. Collegeville, MN: Liturgical Press, 1981. Written by a down-to-earth scholar living in a small cottage on the Welsh/English border (also a former history lecturer at Cambridge University, and a Celtic Christianity expert). A classic.

————. *Seeking God: The Way of St. Benedict*. 2nd edition, Collegeville, MN: Liturgical Press, 2001. Discusses how to make the *Rule* work in modern lives.

Watson, J. S. trans. *Cicero on Oratory and Orators*. NY: Harper and Brothers, 1875. Continues to shed light on Cicero's thought.

Wickham, Chris. *Early Medieval Italy: Central power and local society, 400–1000*. Ann Arbor: University of Michigan Press, 1989. Historical analysis of Benedict's society.

Zimmerman, Odo John and Benedict R. Avery, trans. *Gregory the Great: Life and Miracles of St. Benedict* (Book II, *Dialogues*). Westport, CT: Reprint. Greenwood Press, Publishers, 1980. A reprint of an excellent, scholarly translation published by St. John's Abbey Press (Collegeville, MN, 1949).

ACKNOWLEDGMENTS

Behind every book is a community. The roots of this one are deep in Seoul. During a Fulbright Lectureship, my family and I were at home in this city of 12,000,000 because of the kind Mrs. Shim, Jai-ok; her Fulbright staff; Dr. Cho, Sook-whan; and the English department at Sogang University. They gave us azure joys, like a January visit to the Blue House, and they helped us heal a daughter's broken wrist and, later, a son's double pneumonia. A special 감사합니다 ("Kamsamnida") also to the intelligent Sogang University librarians. They made my daily climb up the gingko-yellow, later snowy, and, finally, red-azalea-stippled hill to Loyola Library worthwhile.

Likewise, Shorter College librarians Dean Kimmetha Herndon, Bettie Sumner, John Rivest, and DeWayne Williams provided support, at first long-distance via the Internet, and most recently over coffee and chocolate muffins. Harold Newman, President of Shorter College, and Provost H. William "Bill" Rice made this book infinitely more possible by creating the position of Scholar-in-Residence, giving me more time to write. George Thomason's Edwardian wit and management talents as Chair have freed me to create, and Terry Morris kindly opened his invaluable medieval history library to me.

Everyone at Paraclete Press deserves my profoundest gratitude, especially the wise Jon Sweeney, Sister Mercy Minor, Jennifer Lynch, Lil Copan, Ron Minor, and Sister

Antonia Cleverly. My husband, Sean, contributed his expertise by designing the unique map of Benedict's Italy and also www.carmenbutcher.com. Like Benedict, he is a man of peace. He is also my sine qua non. And to those who put rubber mice on my pillow, Kate and John, I love you, always, for many splendid reasons, but, most of all (as you already know), "just because."

ABOUT PARACLETE PRESS

WHO WE ARE

Paraclete Press is an ecumenical publisher of books and recordings on Christian spirituality. Our publishing represents a full expression of Christian belief and practice—from Catholic to Evanglical, from Protestant to Orthodox.

Paraclete Press is the publishing arm of the Community of Jesus, an ecumenical monastic community in the Benedictine tradition. As such, we are uniquely positioned in the marketplace without connection to a large corporation and with informal relationships to many branches and denominations of faith.

We like it best when people buy our books from booksellers, our partners in successfully reaching as wide an audience as possible.

WHAT WE ARE DOING
Books

Paraclete Press publishes books that show the richness and depth of what it means to be Christian. Although Benedictine spirituality is at the heart of all that we do, we publish books that reflect the Christian experience across many cultures, time periods, and houses of worship.

We publish books that nourish the vibrant life of the church and its people–books about spiritual practice, formation, history, ideas, and customs.

We have several different series of books within Paraclete Press, including the bestselling *Living Library* series of modernized classic texts; *A Voice from the Monastery*—giving voice to men and women monastics about what it means to live a spiritual life today; award winning literary faith fiction; and books that explore Judaism and Islam and discover how these faiths inform Christian thought and practice.

Recordings

From Gregorian chant to contemporary American choral works, our music recordings celebrate the richness of sacred choral music through the centuries. Paraclete is proud to distribute the recordings of the internationally acclaimed choir Gloriæ Dei Cantores, who have been praised for their "rapt and fathomless spiritual intensity" by *American Record Guide*, and the Gloriæ Dei Cantores Schola, which specializes in the study and performance of Gregorian chant. Paraclete is also the exclusive North American distributor of the Monastic Choir of St. Peter's Abbey in Solesmes, France, long considered to be a leading authority on Gregorian chant performance.

Learn more about us at our Web site:
www.paracletepress.com, or call us toll-free at
1-800-451-5006.

OTHER BENEDICTINE TITLES FROM PARACLETE PRESS

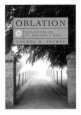

Oblation
Meditations on St. Benedict's Rule
By Rachel Srubas
$14.95
Trade Paper
128 pages
1-55725-488-5

Thousands of spiritual seekers are discovering the wisdom of Saint Benedict. With the grace of a poet, Rachel Srubas writes these uplifting, thought-provoking reflections out of her own experiences of learning the *Rule*, and incorporating it into her "secular' life.

"*Oblation* (from the Latin meaning an offering to God) is a generous offering for anyone seeking God in the spirit of Benedict's Rule."—Br. Benet Tvedten, author of *How to Be a Monastic and Not Leave Your Day Job*

How to Be a Monastic and Not Leave Your Day Job
An Invitation to Oblate Life
By Br. Benet Tvedten
$14.95
Trade Paper
144 pages
1-55725-449-4

You don't have to live in a monastery in order to live like a monk! Oblates are everyday people with jobs, families, and other responsibilities. Sometimes they are Catholic, sometimes not. In today's hectic, changing world, being an oblate offers a rich spiritual connection to the stability and wisdom of an established monastic community.

"A delightful, dry sense of humor. Highly recommended." —Terrence G. Kardong, editor of the *American Benedictine Review*

St. Benedict
Solesmes
$16.95
Gregorian Chant/Organ CD
1-55725-098-7

The father of organized Western monasticism is celebrated with Mass and Office chants and organ music.

Available from most bookstores or through Paraclete Press:
www.paracletepress.com; 1-800-451-5006
Try your local bookstore first.